The Daycare Myth

The Daycare Myth

What We Get Wrong About Early Care and Education (and What We Should Do About It)

Dan Wuori

Foreword by Dana Suskind

TEACHERS COLLEGE PRESS

TEACHERS COLLEGE | COLUMBIA UNIVERSITY
NEW YORK AND LONDON

Published by Teachers College Press,® 1234 Amsterdam Avenue, New York, NY 10027

Library of Congress Cataloging-in-Publication Data

Names: Wuori, Dan, author. | Suskind, Dana, author of foreword.
Title: The daycare myth : what we get wrong about early care and education
    (and what we should do about it) / Dan Wuori ; foreword by Dana Suskind.
Description: New York : Teachers College Press, [2024] | Includes bibliographical
    references and index. | Summary: "This title makes the case for why the early
    years matter; why America's longstanding early childhood policy approach
    sacrifices the needs of young children in favor of promoting adult employment;
    and why fixing the problem makes good sense"—Provided by publisher.
Identifiers: LCCN 2024013604 (print) | LCCN 2024013605 (ebook) |
    ISBN 9780807786482 (paper ; acid-free paper) | ISBN 9780807786499
    (hardcover; acid-free paper) | ISBN 9780807782781 (ebook)
Subjects: LCSH: Early childhood education—United States. | Child care—
    Government policy—United States. | Early childhood educators—Training of—
    United States. | Early childhood education—Parent participation—
    United States.
Classification: LCC LB1139.23 .W86 2024 (print) | LCC LB1139.23 (ebook) |
    DDC 372.210973—dc23/eng/20240531
LC record available at https://lccn.loc.gov/2024013604
LC ebook record available at https://lccn.loc.gov/2024013605

ISBN 978-0-8077-8648-2 (paper)
ISBN 978-0-8077-8649-9 (hardcover)
ISBN 978-0-8077-8278-1 (ebook)

Printed on acid-free paper
Manufactured in the United States of America

For my parents, Don and Joanne, who have set lifelong examples of kindness and service to children. And to Christi, Ben, and Amelia, my everything.

Contents

Foreword

There are few people in the world who could invite me to Arizona in August *and* Alaska in February and reasonably expect me to accept. Indeed, outside of my children, I think the number stands at one: Dan Wuori.

Despite my grumblings about extreme temperatures, those visits to Alaska and Arizona, and a handful of other trips across the nation, all organized by Dan, stand out as some of my favorites of my career. These were trips dedicated to helping state leaders understand, embrace, and act upon the revolutionary science of early childhood development. And unlike most meetings of the sort that I attend, the convenings hosted by Dan in his role as The Hunt Institute's founding Director of Early Learning weren't populated by a room full of like-minded individuals.

To be clear, my respect and admiration for early childhood practitioners and advocates knows no bounds. They are my people, my friends, and I never regret time spent with them. And yet, I recognize that for too long, too many of us have been preaching to the choir, while the rest of the parishioners allow their eyes to glaze over and their minds to wander. "I don't have to worry about that kid stuff," they convince themselves—because their partner had the luxury of leaving the workforce to stay home with their little ones, or because they aren't interested in having children of their own, or because their children are grown, or for any other number of misguided reasons.

Dan is able to cut through those misconceptions better than anyone else I know. He is able to fill a table or a room with passionate advocates and cautious skeptics alike. Because he knows—he deeply believes—that many of us from across our nation's wide social and political spectrum want the same thing—we simply express it in different ways. Dan sees the good in all people and in all efforts to support children and families. And he is uniquely suited to help guide individuals' good intentions, their desire to do right by children, in ways that align with the science of early childhood development.

I have seen elected officials and community leaders of all backgrounds respond to Dan's well-reasoned arguments by adopting his evidence-based recommendations. From advising on governance structures, to the reform of child care systems, prekindergarten, and the optimal use of public and private funds, Dan has brought his expertise to bear with countless American policymakers, advising governors, state lawmakers, and administrative officials on the best path forward—not only for children, but for taxpayers.

Though I've known Dan for more than a decade, I've had the pleasure of working with him more frequently in recent years, thanks to our friends at the Saul Zaentz Charitable Foundation—where Dan serves as Strategic Advisor on Early Childhood—bringing us together to examine the challenges facing American families with young children. One of the biggest, of course, is our nation's broken child care system. With the industry teetering on the edge of collapse—through no fault of the dedicated educators or administrators who populate our ever-dwindling number of child care and early education programs—we have no choice but to fundamentally reimagine the system.

With this book, Dan helps us do so. He not only identifies the myth at the heart of our system, but he empowers us, as readers, to help correct it. It has arrived not a moment too soon. I believe with my whole heart that heeding the recommendations of this volume is a moral and economic imperative.

As a physician and a researcher, I find the scientific evidence presented in these pages compelling. I recognize Dan's signature way of making the science feel accessible and actionable. But in his usual way, he also reminds us of the *magic* inherent in early childhood. And that is what makes *The Daycare Myth* impossible to ignore.

Dana Suskind, MD
Professor of Surgery and Pediatrics, University of Chicago
Co-director, TMW Center for Early Learning + Public Health
Author of *Thirty Million Words*, *Parent Nation*, and
The Scale-Up Effect in Early Childhood and Public Policy

Acknowledgments

The content of this book reflects my learning across decades in the field of early childhood education and is informed by significant mentors who have guided and supported me along the way. I am deeply indebted to Charlene Herring and David Foster, who first saw my promise as a teacher; Dr. Valerie Truesdale, who invited me to bring my knowledge to bear not on a single classroom full of children, but dozens; Susan DeVenny, who taught me virtually everything I know about developing bipartisan support among policymakers; and former North Carolina Governor Jim Hunt and Dr. Javaid Siddiqi, who allowed me the opportunity to put this knowledge to work across the nation.

I'd like to extend my deepest thanks to Sarah Jubar at Teachers College Press (TCP), who had the foresight to make me put this all down on paper and made my experience as a first-time author almost entirely pain-free—as well as to Mike Olivo, who oversaw production, and Jennifer Feldman, publisher of TCP, for her unwavering support of this project. Dave Strauss, TCP's creative director, was the visual genius responsible for this book's cover, which I've loved from the first moment, and Abby Naqvi, Emily Fryer, and Nancy Power all played important roles in marketing the book you now hold in your hands. Without them, who knows if you'd even know it exists?

I am lucky to be represented by Janklow and Nesbit Associates' Hafizah Geter, who also recognized my promise as a writer and has offered me consistently sage advice and thought partnership in the run-up to this book's release.

Thanks as well to Elliot Steinberg, Dan Fortman, Jeana Ross, and the amazing media team at the Saul Zaentz Charitable Foundation for their unwavering support of me, this project, and young children everywhere.

I am indebted to Connecticut Early Childhood Commissioner Beth Bye and Dr. Dana Suskind, co-director of the TMW Center for Early Learning + Public Health at the University of Chicago, who both offered critical feedback on this book at its proposal stage. Special thanks to Dr. Suskind—whom I admire endlessly for her vision to reimagine ours as a "Parent Nation" (in which all families have access to the knowledge and supports they need to thrive)—for writing this book's foreword.

Last but certainly not least, my undying love and gratitude to my wife, Christi, and children, Ben and Amelia, as well as to my parents, Don and Joanne, and sisters, Elisa and Ellen, who have loved and supported me since my own early childhood. May all children experience the same.

The Daycare Myth

CHAPTER 1

Daycare Doesn't Exist

In 1992, the U.S. Department of Agriculture released one of the decade's most ubiquitous and influential images: the Food Pyramid (Figure 1.1). The diagram was designed to provide pictorial guidance on the ideal American diet, with its broad base populated by foods encouraged as healthy dietary staples and its uppermost peak depicting those recommended for limited consumption—or, ideally, avoided altogether.

Figure 1.1. USDA Food Pyramid (1992)

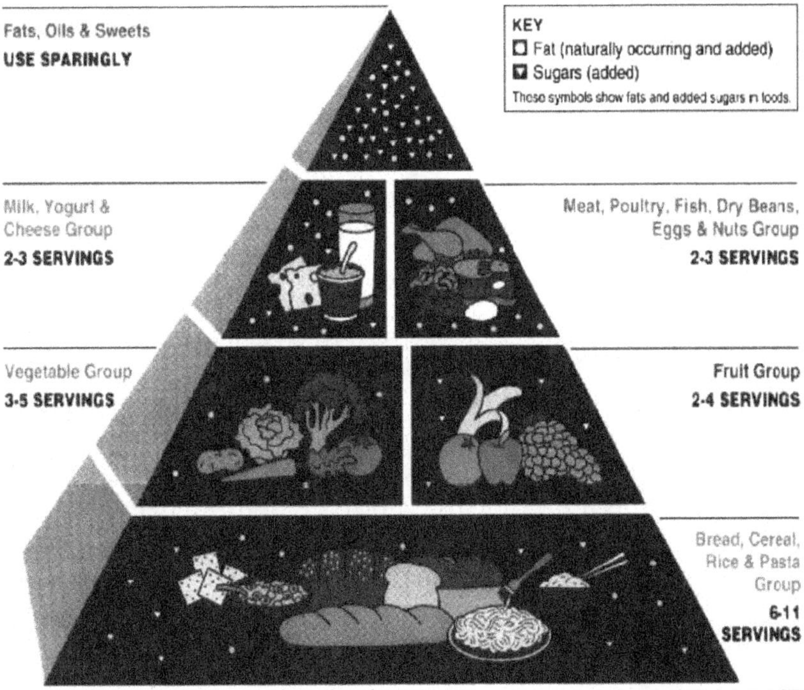

Fats, Oils & Sweets
USE SPARINGLY

KEY
☐ Fat (naturally occurring and added)
☑ Sugars (added)
These symbols show fats and added sugars in foods.

Milk, Yogurt & Cheese Group
2-3 SERVINGS

Meat, Poultry, Fish, Dry Beans, Eggs & Nuts Group
2-3 SERVINGS

Vegetable Group
3-5 SERVINGS

Fruit Group
2-4 SERVINGS

Bread, Cereal, Rice & Pasta Group
6-11 SERVINGS

1

While the pyramid made for a useful graphic organizer in concept, the nutritional guidance it advanced is almost shocking by modern-day standards. At its foundation, with a suggested 6–11 servings per day, were carbohydrates: bread, cereal, rice, and pasta. And at its top—to be banished from the menu alongside sweets—were oils and fats, which narrowly beat out proteins like beef, chicken, and fish on the federal government's healthy eating hit list.

There are, of course, important nuances to be understood about each of these food groups. We know that slow-digesting (complex) carbohydrates are preferable to their highly refined counterparts. And that certain fats are far healthier than others. But there is little question that today's science finds itself squarely at odds with the 1992 pyramid. Indeed, it is difficult to imagine a modern nutritionist advising 10 or more servings of bread and pasta a day as the secret to healthy weight management, all the while eschewing lean proteins and heart-healthy fats like those found in olive oil and avocados.

Just how badly did the USDA miss its mark? In 2008, Harvard University's T. H. Chan School of Public Health issued a revised diagram (Harvard's Healthy Eating Pyramid, Figure 1.2) that *literally inverted* much of the government's original guidance—moving white bread, rice, and pasta from the diagram's welcoming base straight to its ill-advised peak, and healthy fats and oils from its tippy top to a reconfigured base, expanded to emphasize daily exercise and weight control.

Ironically, the 1992 pyramid may *actually have contributed* to the very obesity epidemic it sought to help curb. More than 30 years after its introduction, the graphic stands as both a cautionary tale and a relic of its time—its guidance premised on what we've since come to recognize as a set of outdated and erroneous understandings.

Hindsight is 20/20, as they say. But the pyramid's once-outsized influence on our national behavior raises a troubling question for modern readers: *Where else might we still be getting things boldly and catastrophically wrong?*

The list is almost certain to be lengthy. But at its top, this book will argue, is our nation's public policy approach to young children, their families, and the professionals who serve them. Indeed, American early childhood policy has—for decades—been premised on a myth, the cost of which remains virtually incalculable. Costly to children. Costly to taxpayers. And costly to society as a whole.

This is the myth of daycare, which—in reality—simply doesn't exist.

Figure 1.2. Harvard's Healthy Eating Pyramid (2008)

THE HEALTHY EATING PYRAMID

Department of Nutrition, Harvard School of Public Health

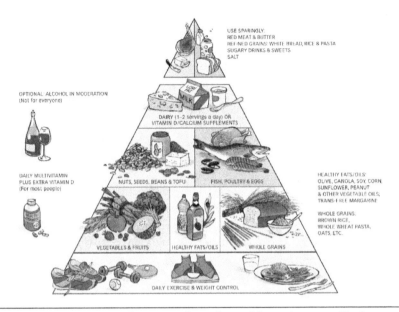

USE SPARINGLY:
RED MEAT & BUTTER
REFINED GRAINS: WHITE BREAD, RICE & PASTA
SUGARY DRINKS & SWEETS
SALT

OPTIONAL: ALCOHOL IN MODERATION
(Not for everyone)

DAIRY (1-2 servings a day) OR
VITAMIN D/CALCIUM SUPPLEMENTS

DAILY MULTIVITAMIN
PLUS EXTRA VITAMIN D
(For most people)

NUTS, SEEDS, BEANS & TOFU   FISH, POULTRY & EGGS

HEALTHY FATS/OILS:
OLIVE, CANOLA, SOY, CORN,
SUNFLOWER, PEANUT
& OTHER VEGETABLE OILS;
TRANS-FREE MARGARINE

WHOLE GRAINS:
BROWN RICE,
WHOLE WHEAT PASTA,
OATS, ETC.

VEGETABLES & FRUITS   HEALTHY FATS/OILS   WHOLE GRAINS

DAILY EXERCISE & WEIGHT CONTROL

Copyright 2008. For more information about the Healthy Eating Pyramid, please see The Nutrition Source, Department of Nutrition, Harvard T.H. Chan School of Public Health, www.thenutritionsource.org, and Eat, Drink, and Be Healthy by Walter C. Willett, M.D. and Patrick J. Skerrett (2005), Free Press/Simon and Schuster Inc.

You read that right: *Daycare doesn't exist.* And I don't mean it's in short supply and difficult to access. I mean it literally. Conceptually. As in, it isn't a thing.

This revelation may come as a particular surprise to those of you shelling out a thousand or more dollars a month to a brick-and-mortar business billing itself as such. And if you fall into this category, you've picked up the right book—because the consequences of these investments could have long-lasting implications for your child's academic and life success.

If, on the other hand, you work in the field, it's possible you're already nodding along. The truth is that the term *daycare* is falling rapidly out of fashion in favor of what most believe to be a slightly more enlightened description: *child care.*

"I don't care for days. I care for children," you may have heard teachers explain of the updated terminology.

And while this is true—and at least an incremental step in the right direction—I'm going to argue that the term *child care* is every bit as worthy of banishment from our collective vocabulary—a concept just as pernicious and divorced from reality as *daycare* itself.

Allow me to explain.

A CRISIS OF UNDERSTANDING

Over the course of this book, I will make the case that America's early childhood sector finds itself mired in a series of interconnected crises: a workforce crisis, a crisis in its economic model, and a crisis of respect, just to name a few.

But here at the outset I want to begin by unpacking the single most consequential crisis facing the field—consequential not only because it is the least discussed, but also because it is the root cause of each of the other crises . . . the patient zero of our current dysfunction. And that is a fundamental *crisis of understanding*.

You see, for decades American public policy has been structured around the premise that child care is somehow *separate and distinct from education*. School—the logic dictates—is a place for learning, whereas care is a support to working families—an industrialized form of baby-sitting that allows parents to earn a living, secure in the knowledge that their children are safe, warm, and well-nourished in their absence.

"Safe, warm, and well-nourished" are important goals in and of themselves—and so it is important to be clear from the outset that my intention is not to disparage the concept of care. For young children, care is life-giving. And can be lifesaving. Children need our care in abundance.

But care is also a low bar, focused by definition on the basic health, safety, and well-being of children, rather than their optimal development. Where we have strayed from the path is in allowing the notion to perpetuate that *care is the sole purpose* of our nation's early childhood settings, when in fact it is but one of many. Care for young children is necessary but not sufficient.

Ultimately, this is the problem with both "daycare" and "child care" as labels. Each centers the concept of care in ways that minimize both the life-altering promise of these settings and the urgency of the American public to act accordingly. In doing so, they advance a false narrative with vast consequences, both human and economic.

That the early years are for caring—and not education—is a notion long (if mostly inadvertently) perpetuated by policymakers. Even those seeking to advance investments in early childhood are prone to framing their arguments around a desire that children *"come to kindergarten ready to learn"*—as if *this* is when and where learning begins. But like the Food Pyramid before it, this logic finds itself in conflict with modern science—and in ways that almost certainly counteract desired outcomes.

Learning Begins in Utero

The question of when learning actually does begin is central to debunking the Daycare Myth. And though this book is not intended as a neuroscience primer (of which there are many, written by vastly more qualified authorities), suffice it to say that learning does not start at age 5, upon entry into a state-funded kindergarten classroom. (Nor, incidentally, does it begin at age 4—as advocacy for expanded public prekindergarten might lead some to conclude.)

The truth is that even the suggestion children are *born learning* doesn't quite capture the reality here. In fact, a growing body of evidence suggests that the earliest forms of learning happen *in utero*, weeks and even months before birth.

As their hearing becomes functional around 18 weeks of gestation, babies begin hearing their earliest sounds within the womb, including their mothers' heartbeat, voice, and digestive rumblings (de Bellefonds, 2021). By 27–30 weeks, they are hearing external sounds as well, to include the voices of others and the sounds of their mothers' immediate environments (muffled though these sounds may yet be).

How do we know that children are learning from what they hear in utero? Amazing research from the University of Washington (McElroy, 2013) suggests that only hours after birth children can not only distinguish—but prefer—the sounds and patterns of their mothers' native languages, which they demonstrate in their differential sucking response rates.

But that's not all. Separate findings from a Finnish research team (Partanen et al., 2013) suggest that babies repeatedly exposed to the lullaby *Twinkle, Twinkle, Little Star* while in utero had distinct neural responses to the tune, both immediately after birth and 4 months later, when compared to a control group without such exposure. Separate findings even suggest that infants may have preferential soothing responses to the familiar themes of television programs to which they were regularly exposed by their mothers during gestation (Hepper, 1988).

More recently, Mariani and colleagues (2023) studied a cohort of 33 newborns, each with a French-speaking mother (and therefore exposed to the rhythms and patterns of the language in utero). Shortly after birth, participating infants' brain waves were monitored using encephalography (EEG) as researchers exposed them to French-, English-, and Spanish-language versions of the classic children's story *Goldilocks and the Three Bears*. Researchers found that their neural activity spiked during the French reading, with infants exhibiting increased long-range temporal correlations (brain waves associated with speech perception and processing) not evidenced during exposure to the English and Spanish versions. In short, the children of French-speaking mothers appear to have already begun organizing the brain's metaphorical circuitry around the French language, even before birth.

This growing body of evidence regarding prenatal learning aligns with decades of research on the developing brain that now conclusively points to the earliest years of life—and *the window from prenatal to age 3, in particular*—as the single most consequential period in all of human development. It is during this time that the fundamental architecture of the brain is "wired" in ways that will either support or hinder the academic and life success of children for decades to come (Brain Architecture, n.d.).

At birth, babies are born with an estimated 100 billion neural cells—nearly all they will ever have—but with limited connections between them (Ackerman, 1992). What we commonly refer to as *brain development* is, accordingly, not so much a process of quantitative growth, but instead about development of the metaphorical circuitry that connects these cells, allowing communication signals to pass between them.

During the earliest years of life, these connections (known as synapses) occur at an astonishing rate, estimated by the Center on the Developing Child at Harvard University at more than one million per second (see Figure 1.3).

As a result, the brain's primary pathways for vision, hearing, language, and higher cognitive function are all largely established by the child's first birthday, with each process already in rapid decline well in advance of kindergarten entry.

For the purposes of our discussion, it's not simply *when* this development happens that matters, but also *how* it occurs. The strength of our neural connections is highly dependent on our early experiences—and in particular the quality of our *interactions with stable, nurturing*

Figure 1.3. Human Brain Development (Charles A. Nelson III, PhD/Harvard Center on the Developing Child)

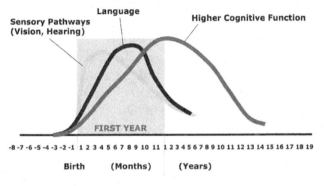

Courtesy of Charles A. Nelson III, PhD.

adults, both inside and outside of the home. Every word spoken, every facial expression, and every experience provided is an opportunity to optimize the brain development of young children—and testament to the critical importance of both parents and the nation's early childhood workforce.

The bottom line is this: For young children, *all environments are learning environments*—which is why the Daycare Myth is so pernicious. Premised on wildly outdated assumptions, America's early childhood systems revolve not around the well-documented reality that early childhood classrooms are humankind's most important learning laboratories—but rather on a misguided belief that they are something of far lesser significance: settings in which custodial care is not only acceptable, but the raison d'etre.

It's only fair to clarify that this misconception is not widely shared by those employed in the field. The nation's early childhood workforce labors tirelessly in the interest of young children, for abysmally poor compensation—which is itself a result of the Daycare Myth. But a careful look at the history and structure of America's public policy investments makes clear that *our systems* have long been designed with the interests of parents—and not children—in mind.

In the world of politics, it's said that a government's true priorities can best be discerned through an analysis of where and how it expends its limited resources. So, let's turn for a moment to when, why, and how the United States has invested—*at least ostensibly*—in young children.

America's Early Childhood Investments as a Means to an End

Our nation has a long history of public investment in early childhood.
   Or . . . does it?
The question is an important one—and central to unraveling the Daycare Myth—because it forces much-needed introspection around what American taxpayers have actually been buying and why.

The United States' first public investment in child care, for example, dates back nearly a century to President Franklin D. Roosevelt's Emergency Nursery School Program (ENSP). The initiative was created in 1933, serving an estimated 72,000 children annually at the peak of its 9-year run (Bipartisan Policy Center, 2019). And what was the program's rationale?

Alongside a plethora of other New Deal programs, the ENSP was intended—first and foremost—to help lift America out of the Great Depression. The Roosevelt administration sought to do so through the creation of sweeping new employment opportunities via its Works Progress Administration. In order for parents to accept this employment, their children required care—hence the federal government's first recorded investment. In short, the ENSP wasn't actually an investment in children per se, as much as it was a means to an altogether different end.

What's followed has been 9 decades of more or less the same. Under a variety of names and iterations, the federal government has "invested in child care" primarily as a support to parental employment, and not as a direct support to enrolled children themselves. (Head Start, launched as an 8-week summer program by the Johnson administration's Office of Economic Opportunity in 1965, stands as perhaps the only notable, child-focused exception to this rule.)

With this as context, you probably won't be surprised to learn that the nation's current Child Care and Development Block Grant (CCDBG, authorized in 1990) was created in much the same vein. Administered by the states under a variety of local names, the CCDBG was always designed to provide child care subsidies to *working* families, but its emphasis on employment was sharpened still further by Congress's welfare-to-work reforms of the mid-1990s.

In 1996, the Personal Responsibility and Work Opportunity Reconciliation Act repealed Roosevelt's Aid to Families with Dependent Children (AFDC—a cash welfare support program for low-income families), replacing it with the newly recast Temporary Assistance for Needy Families (TANF). Focused on time-limited benefits and incorporating aggressive new work requirements, the new welfare structure eliminated AFDC's child care entitlement, while reauthorizing CCDBG under a new structure focused on lifting families out of poverty through self-sufficiency.

All told, the United States' investments in child care have had surprisingly little to do with children. This doesn't diminish the importance of parental employment, as either a legitimate public policy goal or as a family support unto itself. But it's time we got honest—not only about what we're actually paying for—but about *how the federal government's adult-focused approach has shaped our very conception of the early years.*

Public Policy's Greatest Mismatch

This brings us to American public policy's most catastrophic mismatch between *what we know* and *what we do*. In spite of decades of science to the contrary, we continue to lull ourselves into accepting that our nation's most important learning environments simply . . . *aren't for learning.*

One of the most egregious examples of this disconnect came in October 2021, as President Joe Biden announced the broad strokes of what would become his ill-fated Build Back Better agenda. Just minutes after speaking to the need to expand access to affordable child care, the president turned his attention to a companion plan to create universal prekindergarten, taking pains to clarify that the latter would be "school, not daycare . . . school."

Watching him that night, it wasn't my sense that the president meant to denigrate programs serving the nation's youngest children, but instead that he—like so much of American society—had fallen victim to the Daycare Myth, accepting as fact the notion that it is possible (and in this case, apparently, *necessary*) to separate care from learning.

The truth is that the two simply *can't be separated.* Once we accept that learning begins in utero and that the long-term academic and life success of children depends on optimizing brain development during

the earliest months and years, we are through the looking glass . . . and
finally staring clear-eyed at the catastrophe we have created (and continue to sustain without examination) for the nation's young children.

How far *are* we from the system we actually need? The terrifying
reality is that our current system is not unlike the 1992 Food Pyramid:
in need of a literal inversion.

This is a process this book hopes to kickstart by equipping parents,
providers, and policymakers with the knowledge needed to effect change.
In an effort to begin the conversation, let's take a moment to unpack the
implications of what we know, beginning with three of the most salient
takeaways we've discussed thus far. These points, which I'll refer to as
The Three Simple Truths of Early Development—or simply *The Three Simple
Truths*—throughout the remainder of this book, are as follows:

The Three Simple Truths of Early Development

(1) Learning begins in utero and never stops.
(2) The period from prenatal to age 3 is a uniquely consequential
     window of human development during which the fundamental
     architecture of the brain is "wired."
(3) Optimal brain development is dependent on stable, nurturing
     relationships with highly engaged adults.

Can We Develop Public Policy Based on the Three Truths?

What might our early childhood policy look like if we accepted *The
Three Truths* as its revised basis?

It would begin with a fundamental rethinking of our attitudes
toward everything from prenatal health to young children themselves.
No longer viewed primarily as a caregiving task, the optimal development of infants and toddlers would become a strategic priority for
the nation with far-reaching implications, not only for young children
and their families, but for taxpayers and our collective prosperity. (In
Chapter 2, we'll unpack how proactive investment in young children
may actually be our most realistic—and responsible—opportunity to
promote self-sufficiency and *shrink the size of government*.)

Policy grounded in *The Three Simple Truths* would also necessitate a
renewed emphasis on the role of parents, particularly during the first

year of life—promoting robust conversation about not only paid family leave, but how American public policy might be appropriately re-shaped to incentivize parenting over workforce participation (among those willing and able to choose this path) during humankind's most formative window of development. Currently an estimated 67% of American children under the age of 6 reside in households in which all available adults participate in the workforce (Kids Count Data Center, 2021b). What's less understood is how many of these parents do so out of sheer economic necessity, and how this figure might shift given more family-friendly policies focused on strengthening parental bonds and optimizing early development. I'll unpack this idea in greater de-tail in Chapter 5.

Whether in the home or in the classroom, policy based on *The Three Simple Truths* would demand a renewed focus on adult learning, ensur-ing that those impacting young children's lives have the requisite child development knowledge and skills needed to maximize the once-in-a-lifetime opportunity with which they have been entrusted. It would also be focused on continuity, incentivizing—*in part through professional wages and benefits* for those working in the field—the creation of sus-tained and deeply personalized relationships between children and their most significant adults.

In the classroom, such policy would translate to developmen-tally appropriate, evidence-based curriculum; an expanded focus on the language development that undergirds everything from written literacy to human cognition itself; and a broad-based approach to supporting the needs of young children across multiple domains of development.

In short, it would look nothing like the early childhood policy of today.

The Realities of Having Children in America Today

Indeed, if one's goal was to create a bizarro world in which *The Three Simple Truths* were deliberately and systematically undermined (rather than consciously promoted), they'd be hard-pressed to come up with a system any more backward than the one American parents are cur-rently left to navigate daily.

If that sounds hyperbolic, consider the reality of childbirth in our country. As I write these words, 1 in 5 American mothers receives no prenatal care during the first trimester of pregnancy, with more than 1 in 20 American children born to mothers who received *late or no prenatal care whatsoever* (Kids Count Data Center, 2021a).

After a child is born, things get even worse. With 81% of American parents unable to access paid family leave, an astonishing 1 in 4 new mothers is forced to return to work *less than 2 weeks* after giving birth (Bipartisan Policy Center, 2020a). During humankind's most critical period of bonding—the very weeks and months during which trust, love, and connectivity are formed between mother and baby—ours is, again, a society in which the work of adults is privileged above the brain development of children.

We can only speculate as to the long-term costs paid by children and taxpayers due to our abject and persistent failure to welcome babies into a world where their development is honored as both a moral imperative and a high-yield investment. As parents know painfully well, however, these costs are much easier to calculate at the household level.

The average yearly tuition within the nation's early childhood education programs (which is the label I will endeavor to use from here on out in place of daycare/child care, which—again—don't exist) now stands at $14,117 according to one recent analysis (Thier, 2022). In 28 states this cost actually exceeds that of in-state college tuition at public universities, an expense many families struggle to afford even after saving for the first 17 years of their child's life (Patel, 2023).

But wait, you might insist. Isn't this cost subsidized for low-income families via the Child Care and Development Block Grant? For a lucky few, the answer is yes. But it is important to keep in mind that (due to chronic underinvestment) only 1 in 7 income-eligible families actually receives subsidy support, leaving over half of families with young children paying more than 20% of their annual family incomes (U.S. Government Accountability Office, 2021).

What do they get for this amount? In most cases, far less than *The Three Simple Truths* would dictate. Lulled into a false sense that these programs exist to provide caretaking rather than brain-building, American parents purchase the quality they can afford, if they are lucky enough to be able to access a space at all.

Who staffs these classrooms? In most cases the answer, sadly, is not highly credentialed child development specialists. During precisely the period that science dictates the need for stable, nurturing relationships with engaged adults, we provide instead a revolving door of minimally qualified staff, paid at or near their states' minimum wages—59 cents less per hour than dog walkers, according to recent data from the U.S. Bureau of Labor Statistics (2022).

It all begs what may be this book's most important question: Why?

Why do we continue clinging to a system we *know* is not right for children?

The multifaceted answer begins with inertia. While brain science has offered us a wealth of new insights over the past several decades, America's early childhood structures and investments in child care as a workforce strategy predate many—if not most—of this literature's most compelling findings.

The other major impediment to a solution appears to be cost. I say "appears to be" because, in truth, American taxpayers are already footing the bill for this crisis. A 2023 report from the business group Ready Nation, for example, estimates that lack of high-quality infant and toddler programs for families results in an annual loss to the American economy of $122 billion (Bishop, 2023).

The bulk of these losses (an estimated $78 billion) are borne by parents in the form of foregone wages and career setbacks. Parents are often late and/or forced to call out of work to address the needs of their children. They refuse—or are bypassed for—promotions and career training that might advance their earning potential due to lack of availability. And in the absence of options for their babies, they are often forced to leave the workforce altogether.

Employers likewise bear the brunt of our early care and education crisis, losing an estimated $23 billion annually. As their employees struggle to meet family needs, productivity and profitability drop. Employers are challenged to recruit and retain staff, incurring the costs of continual rehiring and retraining.

Finally, taxpayers suffer. When parents and employers earn less, state economies are starved of revenues that might otherwise flow into their coffers. Ready Nation pegs this loss at $21 billion annually.

When you couple this with the cost of educational remediation, social services, and interactions with the criminal justice system, all known to correlate with our suboptimization of children's development, the bottom line is plain: We're already paying the cost; we're just doing it in the dumbest possible ways.

It's time for a change.

THE BIPARTISAN BLUEPRINT FOR CHANGE

It is my intent, throughout this book, to do more than uplift the nation's early childhood policy challenges. While a thorough understanding is key to their solution, history has shown that simply *knowing better* does not always translate to *doing better*—especially in cases requiring fundamental shifts in our collective thinking.

Indeed, transforming the nation's early childhood landscape will require collective action. Action from parents. Action from early childhood professionals. And perhaps most importantly, action from policymakers at all levels. In order to advance this cause, each of this book's first four chapters will end with a set of succinct and actionable suggestions for readers in each of these categories: the Bipartisan Blueprint for Change.

Parents

If you take nothing else away from this chapter, let it be this: *Your child's earliest years matter*. The period from prenatal to 3 is the single most consequential window in all of human development, and your child's experiences during these critical years hold the potential to shape their success for decades to come. So, act in accordance with *The Three Simple Truths*. Here's how:

- *Plan ahead.* While not everyone has the luxury of a preplanned pregnancy, know that it's never too early to begin preparing for your life with children. Parenthood is both costly and complex, so beginning with a game plan and the necessary resources to optimize both your baby's well-being and your own is well advised.

  Whether in your home or in a high-quality early childhood education program, your baby will require sustained, attentive, and nurturing interaction with loving adults. Knowing who these adults will be and how you'll be able to afford their provision will position your child for a great start, even before conception.
- *Start early.* Your child's development, well-being, and learning all begin in utero, making early and regular prenatal care and thoughtful nutrition/consumption both critical. Remember that your baby's hearing will become functional during the final trimester, so read, sing, and talk to your baby—and encourage other family members to do the same.
- *Never forget: Daycare doesn't exist.* Contrary to public opinion, there is no distinction between child care and education. Because learning begins in utero and never ceases, *all environments are learning environments for young children.*

The real question is: Is your child in a good one?

Attentive, high-quality interactions are key to your child's brain development—so make this the overriding criterion on which you assess the choices before you. When looking at out-of-home preschool programs, always visit in advance— and not just for a 2-minute walk-through. Spend some time actually observing. As you do, look past the center's décor and materials, and *watch the adults.* How often are they interacting with children—and in what ways? Are they supporting the children's use of language? Are they down on the floor interacting at the children's eye level—or off in a corner chatting with other adults?

Given the choice between a state-of-the-art building and nurturing, attentive adults, go with the adults every time. *This isn't babysitting. These are the people you are literally entrusting to co-construct your child's brain.*

- *Advocate.* Now that you understand the brokenness of our early childhood systems, it is incumbent on you to take action. Speak to your state and local elected leaders (governor's office, state legislators, city and county council members, etc.) about the need for paid family leave and the value of high-quality early childhood education programs for all children. Share your story and your challenges. Be part of a movement for change.

Professionals

Though the information in this chapter will have come as little surprise to many early childhood professionals, the field has a special responsibility to convert this knowledge into practice. Here are the most important ways you can do so:

- *Claim your titles.* Throughout this chapter I've staked the claim that "daycare" and "child care" don't exist as entities separate and distinct from early childhood education. But that reality hasn't stopped a huge percentage of the field from continuing to market and refer to itself using these outdated titles.

  The same holds true for the professionals working in these settings, who—in many cases—continue to hold themselves up as "child care providers" and "daycare workers."

In order for the field to earn the respect and recognition it so richly deserves, it is essential that early childhood professionals take the first step—and claim titles that correspond, not with outdated public perceptions, but with decades of brain science. Facilities in which children learn and grow are *schools,* and the adults that facilitate this learning—independent of compensation or the degrees they hold—are *teachers.* Full stop. No one is going to acknowledge you as such unless and until you do so yourself.

- *Speak your truth.* As we'll establish in future chapters, the early education workforce is in crisis, pairing physically and emotionally demanding work with abysmal pay and, typically, the absence of employer-funded health and retirement benefits. In the same way that it is incumbent on parents to advocate with policymakers, so too must early childhood professionals speak out on their own behalf—strengthening awareness of their important work, needs, and challenges.

Policymakers

Perhaps no one in this conversation holds greater power to effect change than policymakers. Knowing what you now do, here are a few ways you can begin transforming the nation's early childhood policy landscape:

- *Begin a paradigm shift by redefining the early years in statute.* In the same way that parents and professionals must reshape their conceptions of the early years, so too must policymakers. One simple, yet powerful, opportunity to begin this conversation is to enact technical revisions to the laws and regulations governing early childhood education in your jurisdiction, replacing outdated terminology (such as "daycare" and "workers") with language that better reflects the state of our knowledge and science ("early childhood education programs" and "teachers").
- *Enact policy changes designed to better support the families of young children.* Knowing what we do about the importance of the earliest months and years of development, it is unconscionable that 1 in 4 American mothers, for example, must return to work within just 2 weeks after the birth of a child. Robust paid family leave policies (to include adoptive

and foster parents) and access to high-quality, affordable early childhood education programs are essential to the long-term prosperity of both the children in question and our nation itself.

Yes, these programs have a cost. But as we'll unpack in Chapter 2, the cost of our inaction is incalculably higher.

- *Focus on classroom interaction quality.* Over the course of recent decades, many states have implemented—with the best of intentions—quality rating systems designed to support families in the identification of high-quality programs for their children.

Frequently, however, these systems have defined and measured quality in suspect ways—privileging structural indicators of quality (the number of books, the height of sinks, and types of sanitation practices used, to name a few) over the quality of the overall learning environment, including interactions between adults and children, learning activities, and more.

While these structural indicators of quality are impor-tant in and of themselves, they can inadvertently eclipse what matters most in classrooms, fooling parents into believing that well-equipped and visually attractive classrooms are inherently high-quality when they are not.

The best such systems offer a healthy balance between structural and process measures of quality, recognizing that ultimately it is the overall learning environment—which includes *interactions between teachers and children (and among children themselves)* that truly distinguish top-quality classrooms. If you don't know how your state/community defines and measures early childhood quality, find out and ensure that this balance is present.

Something for Everyone
The Bipartisan Case for Early Childhood Investment

In November 2022, New Mexico voters went to the polls for more than your typical statewide election. On the ballot were not just candidates—including Democratic Governor Michelle Lujan Grisham, who was seeking reelection to a second term—but a first-of-its-kind amendment that would enshrine permanent funding for early childhood education in the state's constitution. The ballot measure, which proposed to dedicate an estimated $150 million annually from the state's Land Grant Permanent Fund (derived from New Mexico's booming oil and gas revenues), passed in a landslide, garnering a full 70% of the statewide vote—some 18% more than Governor Lujan Grisham herself (who advanced comfortably with 52% support).

The takeaway: Voters across party lines turned out in force to support the needs of the state's young children.

New Mexico isn't alone in this regard. In a polarized environment in which consensus seems increasingly difficult to come by, voters from across the nation—*and across the political spectrum*—are all-in on children. Indeed, polling on the topic is so lopsided in favor of increased investment that readers might be forgiven for initially approaching these data with the same skepticism with which we greet the "approval" ratings of foreign dictators.

Take Pennsylvania, for example, where a poll commissioned by the Early Learning PA Coalition (2023) found that 98% of registered voters identify early childhood education as important—with nearly 8 out of 10 supporting increased state funding to serve more eligible children in the state's prekindergarten program. Or recent national polling from the First Five Years Fund (2023), in which 90% of Republicans, 93% of Independents, and 96% of Democrats agreed that finding quality child care programs for children of working parents is critical—with

74% expressing support for increased federal child care spending as both an important priority and a "good use of tax dollars."

Here's a challenge: Name another public policy topic on which virtually all voters agree. A place where voters across party lines say, "Hey, we should really spend more on that." I'll wait . . .

Putting aside for a moment our nation's persistent mismatch between *support for* investment and *investment itself,* this chapter will unpack the bipartisan case for early childhood. It is a case for action—which, in a nutshell, boils down to this: *Proactive early childhood investments offer something for everyone.*

Whether you're a dyed-in-the-wool liberal, a hard-core conservative, or somewhere in between, investing in young children just makes good sense. What's more, you'll find that these investments are aligned with your worldview—no matter what space on the political spectrum you may occupy. Over the coming pages I'll unpack a variety of arguments in favor of enacting early childhood policies consistent with *The Three Simple Truths.* Some of these arguments may resonate with you more than others. And that's okay. In fact, it's exactly the point. Feel free to pick and choose among those that speak to you most.

Remember: Something for everyone.

THE LONG-TERM ECONOMIC CASE FOR INVESTMENT IN YOUNG CHILDREN

Suppose for a moment that your financial advisor approached you with an opportunity that offered a reliable 13% annual return on every dollar invested. Chances are that you'd jump at the opportunity. You'd really be crazy not to. After all, the long-term annual return of the Standard and Poor's 500 (S&P 500, a stock market index tracking the performance of 500 of the nation's largest companies) has historically averaged about 10%, with market fluctuations capable of driving this average in either direction during any given year.

Consider the S&P 500's recent 5-, 10-, 20-, and 30-year returns, as reflected in Figure 2.1 (Royal & O'Shea, 2023). While it's important to note that this 2022 data is skewed a bit lower by that year's pandemic-induced economic downturn, the data speak to both the reality of the market's volatility and its challenges to investors—with its 5-, 20-, and 30-year returns topping out at 7.64%, and even its best window (the 10-year period from 2013 to 2022) still yielding well below our hypothetical return on investment (ROI).

Figure 2.1. S&P 500's Recent 5-, 10-, 20-, and 30-Year Returns

Period (start-of-year to end-of-2022)	Average annual S&P 500 return
5 years (2018–2022)	7.51%
10 years (2013–2022)	10.41%
20 years (2003–2022)	7.64%
30 years (1993–2022)	7.52%

Figure 2.2. The Heckman Curve (Heckman, 2006)

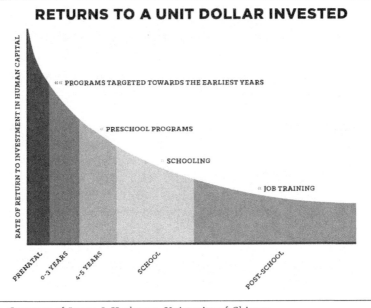

Source: Courtesy of James J. Heckman, University of Chicago

Indeed, 13% would be one heck of a payoff. It's also the very fig-ure Nobel Prize–winning economist James Heckman has documented as the annual ROI to taxpayers derived from investments in high-quality early childhood programs.

Heckman has dedicated much of his career to teasing out the eco-nomic benefits of early childhood interventions. Using longitudinal data from the field's foundational studies, he and his colleagues have followed participant outcomes across decades, building a compelling dollars-and-cents case for early investment.

Figure 2.2, known as "The Heckman Curve" (Heckman, 2006), de-picts the gist of the economist's findings across multiple analyses—a case that can be boiled down to one simple conclusion: *The earlier we invest in high-quality early childhood programs, the greater the return to society.*

Three of Heckman's analyses, conducted over more than a decade, are particularly illuminating in this regard. I'll briefly summarize each below. *(A note here: As we begin digging into some of early childhood's most notable research studies, that I've included a few additional thoughts on interpreting research claims in Appendix A.)*

HighScope's Perry Preschool Project

The first of these studies analyzed the rate of return from HighScope's Perry Preschool Project (Heckman et al., 2010), a classroom-based program serving 123 economically disadvantaged 3- and 4-year-olds in Ypsilanti, Michigan, in the early 1960s. Tracking the academic and life outcomes of participants (alongside those of a matched control group) through the age of 40, Heckman and his coauthors credit the program with a 7% to 10% annual rate of return to society—noting for the non-economists among us that "annual rates of return of this magnitude, if compounded and reinvested annually over a 65-year life, imply that each dollar invested at age four yields a return of 60 to 300 dollars by age 65" (p. 115).

Not a bad deal, right? After all, a 7% to 10% return puts high-quality prekindergarten on par with the S&P 500 as an investment opportunity.

How were these dividends calculated? Heckman and his colleagues found that, when compared to a control group of non-enrolled children, participating preschoolers (and female students, in particular) enjoyed a host of benefits—both as they advanced through school and into their adult lives, demonstrating:

- Substantially higher rates of high school graduation among females (88% vs. 34%);
- Higher rates of employment and superior annual earnings at both ages 27 and 40;
- A near 50% decrease in the number of male participants having accessed welfare at age 40;
- And substantially fewer arrests.

Take just a moment, reread the figures above, and consider the implications of each. An investment that more than doubled high school graduation rates among females. An intervention that cut welfare participation in half and kept adults from entering the criminal justice system. It begs the question: How are we yet to enact such programs at scale?

A separate analysis of Perry's outcomes conducted by Dr. Larry Schweinhart (2005) documented similarly compelling results, finding:

- Diminished rates of treatment for mental health disorders (8% vs. 36% within the control group)
- A roughly 50% decrease in grade-level retention (21% vs. 41%)
- Superior academic achievement at ages 9, 10, and 14, as well as on measures of literacy at ages 19 and 27
- A greater likelihood of home ownership at ages 27 (27% vs. 5%) and 40 (37% vs. 28%)
- Improved odds of possessing a savings account (76% vs. 50%)
- Diminished use of social services at age 27 (59% vs. 80%)
- A near doubling of the number of males raising their own children (57% vs. 30%)

All told, high-quality preschool offers a staggering array of benefits—both to participating children and to taxpayers. But if you return to the Heckman Curve graphic, you'll note that investments in children aged 3 and 4—while demonstrating substantially higher rates of return than K–12 education—still don't come close to delivering the biggest bang for the buck. For that we'll have to start even earlier. So, let's turn for a moment to a second analysis conducted by Heckman and colleagues (Garcia, et al., 2017).

The Carolina Abecedarian Project (ABC) and the Carolina Approach to Responsive Education (CARE)

This second study explored the costs and social benefits derived by a pair of 1970s-era North Carolina early childhood programs: the Carolina Abecedarian Project (ABC) and the Carolina Approach to Responsive Education (CARE). Like Perry Preschool, both were evaluated by randomized control trials, but unlike Perry (which targeted 3- and 4-year-old children), ABC and CARE both began serving children as early as 8 weeks of age, providing high-quality child care alongside comprehensive developmental resources (including nutrition and access to health care) to participating children until kindergarten entry at age 5.

Figure 2.3. Health Effects of Abecedarian Intervention at Age 35 (Campbell et al., 2014)

Indicator	Participant Mean	Control Group Mean
Systolic Blood Pressure	125.79	143.33
Diastolic Blood Pressure	78.53	92.00
Pre-hypertension	0.68	0.78
Hypertension	0.10	0.44
HDL ("Good") Cholesterol	53.21	42.00
Cholesterol/HDL-C	3.89	4.69
Abdominal Obesity	0.65	0.87
Metabolic Syndrome	0.00	0.25

ABC/CARE yielded game-changing educational outcomes similar to those found in the Perry study—with participants demonstrating permanent gains in I.Q. and social-emotional skills, staying in school longer, and achieving superior high school graduation rates. But with the benefit of earlier and more comprehensive services, the North Carolina participants also demonstrated significantly improved health outcomes at age 35, as demonstrated in Figure 2.3.

The inclusion of these advantageous adult health outcomes—alongside improved parental workforce participation stemming from the availability of high-quality child care beginning shortly after birth—led to Heckman's revised 13% annual return on investment figure, well surpassing the estimated 7% to 10% derived from Perry's preschool-only model.

Even here, the story is not yet complete. With the Perry study recently marking 60 years since the enrollment of its first preschool-aged participants, Heckman and his colleagues have now revisited the study's outcomes through age 54 (Garcia et al., 2021), imputing, for the first time, *benefits to both the siblings and children* of the original Perry participants.

Second-Generation Findings From the Perry Preschool Project

In addition to documenting the continuing gains among the study's original participants (which included significant increases in employment; health, cognitive, and socioemotional skills; and reductions in male participants' criminal activity) at age 54, Heckman's most recent analysis found "substantial second generation effects on education, employment, crime, school suspensions and health," noting that the children of participants were "less likely to be suspended from school, and more likely to complete regular or any other form of high school and to be employed full-time with some college experience" at the time of publication (Heckman, 2019, p. 1).

Interestingly, whereas the initial Perry analysis emphasized the disproportionate educational benefits accrued by female participants, Heckman notes that among the children of original participants, benefits are particularly strong for male children—and especially so for the male children of male participants.

The children of Perry participants were more likely than the children of nonparticipants to:

- Complete high school without suspension (67% among children of participants vs. 40% among children of nonparticipants)
- Never have been suspended, addicted, or arrested (60% vs. 40%)
- Be employed full-time or self-employed (59% vs. 42%)

To what might we attribute these positive outcomes? Heckman's (2019) data suggest that high-quality early learning experiences led to more stable and positive family lives in adulthood. In short, Perry participants had more solid marriages and raised their children in more two-parent households—both of which afforded parents the ability to provide the resources and attention necessary to optimize their children's development in alignment with our Three Simple Truths of Early Development.

In the end, Heckman found that children of Perry participants *spent fully 3 times more time with stably married parents* before the age of 18—with this figure increasing to *15 times more* among the male children of male participants.

The bottom line? We are only beginning to understand the long-term, multigenerational benefits associated with investments in early development.

THE SHORT-TERM ECONOMIC CASE FOR INVESTMENT IN YOUNG CHILDREN

While the long-term economic benefits of investment in young children are compelling in and of themselves, they tell only half the story. For the other half, we needn't look decades into the future. Instead, let's look at the real-time consequences of our current inaction on our state and federal economies.

In 2021, a reported 67% of American children under the age of 6 resided in households in which all available parents work outside the home (Kids Count Data Center, 2021b), making affordable and accessible early education programs essential to the workforce participation of millions.

If you're the parent of a young child, however, you know not only how unaffordable and inaccessible these programs can be, but also what a toll their absence can take on your employment, income, and upward mobility. Employers experience similar challenges in reverse, struggling to hire and retain staff and suffering from losses in productivity and profitability as a result of a workforce unable to accommodate the needs of their children.

As briefly referenced in Chapter 1, Council for a Strong America's Ready Nation—an organization of business leaders supportive of increased early childhood investment—recently studied the annual drain on the American economy resulting from a lack of high-quality early education programs for infants and toddlers, pegging this cost at $122 billion a year (Bishop, 2023).

In the context of our national economy, it's easy to grow numb to the magnitude of such figures. Fortunately, Ready Nation's analysis breaks this annual cost down not only by category (losses incurred by parents, businesses, and taxpayers writ large), but also at the individual level. And the figures might surprise you.

The parents of young children bear the most significant share of this burden, accounting for $78 billion (or 64% of the $122 billion total) in annual losses resulting from lost and foregone wages—with this figure equating to $5,520 *per working parent* during each of the years from birth to 3. *This isn't the price of the tuition they're paying to enroll their children, mind you.* These are wages they are missing out on each year because they are late, absent, and/or missing out on beneficial workforce training and promotions as they struggle to meet the early education needs of their young children.

When parents aren't productive employees, the effects are felt within the bottom lines of their employers as well, with businesses estimated to lose out on some $23 billion annually in diminished revenue and extra hiring hosts. For individual employers, this equates to $1,640 per parent employed.

Finally, when both parents and their employers aren't earning as they otherwise would, the impact is felt by taxpayers—independent of whether they themselves are parents of young children. Diminished tax revenues account for $21 billion in annual losses to the states, to the tune of $1,470 per working parent (see Figure 2.4).

Figure 2.4. Economic Impacts on Parents, Employers, and Taxpayers

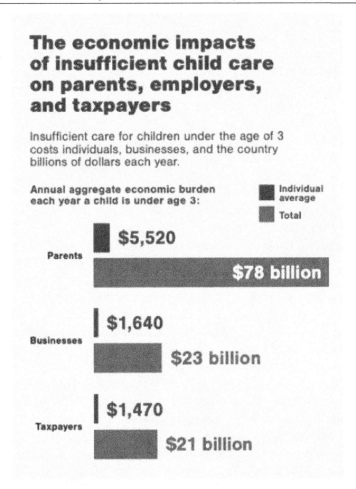

Source: Bishop (2023).

It's worth noting here that, in regard to workforce, investments in high-quality early education programs are, themselves, two-generational. They enable the productivity of the nation's current workforce—driving real-time economic prosperity—while simultaneously preparing its future workforce for success in an increasingly competitive global marketplace.

I mean, really . . . what's not to like?

Turbocharging America's Economy While Shrinking the Size of Government

In 2001, Grover Norquist, the founder and president of Americans for Tax Reform, outlined a vision that would divide the right and left along partisan lines for years to come. Noting that the size of government is the "central question in American politics" (National Public Radio, 2001), the conservative Norquist outlined his ambition to shrink the size of the federal government by 50% over 25 years—punctuating his point with one of the decade's most blunt, yet influential, quips:

> "I don't want to abolish government," Norquist explained. "I simply want to reduce it to the size where I can drag it into the bathroom and drown it in the bathtub."

Norquist's radical vision and graphic imagery did little to endear him to progressives, but his influence loomed large in the years to come—most notably as the creator of a "No New Taxes" pledge that, for more than a decade, became a virtual prerequisite for office among Republican political candidates.

After decades working at the intersection of policy and politics, I'm yet to meet anyone who is a fan of bloated government. Or taxes. The problem with Norquist's vision is ultimately less about its aim and more its short-term practicality. Eliminating half of government would require draconian cuts in services on which Americans depend: Medicaid, Social Security, education, transportation, and national defense, just to name a few. Indeed, so much of the nation's budget is dominated by social safety net programs that the federal government is sometimes derisively—but not altogether inaccurately—referred to as "an insurance program with an army."

But what if there *was* a way to meaningfully advance toward Norquist's vision of smaller government and lower taxes? A way that *didn't* rely on cuts to services—but rather on diminishing our need for them in the first place? What if there was a way to shrink dependence on social services; require less special education, remediation, and retention in our schools; boost family stability; and improve health outcomes?

The truth, as you now know, is that *all of these outcomes (and more)* have been documented in association with investments in high-quality early childhood education—and that's not even accounting for the positive, real-time economic impacts on workforce participation, profitability, and productivity.

Ultimately the economic case for investment in the nation's youngest learners is both compelling and deeply bipartisan, allowing opportunities to meaningfully and concurrently:

- Shrink the size of government and lower taxes.
- Ensure the availability (and sustainability) of a social safety net, while diminishing demand for its services.
- Turbo-charge the American economy, improving workforce participation (among those who wish to do so), increasing employer productivity and profitability, and boosting both individual earnings and state and federal tax revenues.

Strengthening the Nuclear Family

Thus far, Chapter 2 has focused on the significant benefits of classroom-based interventions for young children. But as my colleague Katharine Stevens, founder and CEO of the D.C.-based Center on Child and Family Policy, is always quick to note, early development is not necessarily synonymous with *early school* (ElHage, 2022). And the same holds true for state and federal public policy investments in this space, many of which are rightfully focused on family strengthening and the well-being of parents.

In the United States today, nearly 24 million children reside in single parent households (Annie E. Casey Foundation, 2023). And though many children manage to thrive in these situations, there's little debate as to whether nurturing and stable two-parent households offer greater economic security, fewer stressors/demands, and improved developmental settings.

That's neither a criticism of those who find themselves raising children solo—often for reasons entirely outside of their control—nor a suggestion that children cannot develop optimally in such households. But it is a truth, nonetheless. Single parenthood is hard.

I won't bother to rehash here the family-strengthening benefits documented in the preceding section, but the second-generation findings from the Perry Preschool Project are nonetheless significant and deserve the focused attention of every policymaker interested in strengthening the nuclear family. Independent of the very real economic benefits of these outcomes, they speak to societal well-being and the quality of human existence.

That said, family strengthening is about more than the number of available adults in the household. It also has to do with access to knowledge and resources. Ask any parent and they'll readily admit that none of us—independent of education and professional experience—are ever fully prepared to be first-time parents.

Pediatricians are first-time parents, as are early childhood educators. Might they know more than the average parent as they begin their journeys? Perhaps. But the bottom line is that until you've experienced raising an infant 24 hours a day, well . . . you haven't.

This is one reason why both states and the federal government are increasingly investing in things like evidence-based home visiting programs—through which trained professionals make personalized visits designed to support new parents not only in their knowledge of child development and age-appropriate care routines, but also in their knowledge of other community-based resources available to support them in everything from nutrition to mental health.

One of the field's best researched programs, Nurse-Family Partnership (NFP), matches first-time low-income mothers with registered nurses for home visits beginning during the second trimester of pregnancy and extending until the child's 2nd birthday. Unlike Perry and Abecedarian, NFP is a parent-focused intervention, designed to support new mothers in their own important roles. Like these classroom-based interventions, however, NFP's longitudinal outcomes are significant and hold the promise not only to strengthen families, but to reap substantial rewards to taxpayers.

Better equipped to handle the stresses of parenthood and armed with a vastly improved understanding of their children's development, NFP mother-participants demonstrated a 48% reduction in child abuse and neglect when compared to a matched control group comprised of nonparticipants (Nurse-Family Partnership, 2022). And with regular consultation with program nurses, participants made 56% fewer visits to hospital emergency rooms for child accidents and poisonings.

Additionally, participants' children demonstrated:

- A 50% reduction in language delays at 21 months of age
- 67% less behavioral/intellectual problems at age 6
- A 59% reduction in child arrests at age 15

Participating mothers, meanwhile, demonstrated:

- 32% fewer subsequent pregnancies
- An 82% increase in months employed
- 61% fewer maternal arrests

Given these robust outcomes, it won't surprise you to know that NFP has been subjected to its own rigorous benefit-cost analysis, which found that the program produces state and federal cost savings averaging $26,898 per family served—some 2.9 times the cost of the program itself (Nurse-Family Partnership, 2017). Considering the program's broader savings to society (including potential gains in work, wages, and quality of life) alongside specific cost savings (out-of-pocket payments, including savings on medical care, child welfare, special education, and criminal justice), one analysis (Miller, 2015) pegs NFP's total benefits to society at *$60,428 per family served* (a return of $6.40 for every dollar invested).

Strengthening the Provision of Paid Family Leave

Clearly there are substantial benefits to investing in parents. But a national policy reenvisioned around *The Three Simple Truths* would do more than simply support parents as their children's first and best teachers. It would also allow them greater opportunity to actually do the job in person, beginning with the provision of paid family leave.

As referenced in Chapter 1, an astonishing 1 in 4 American mothers is forced to return to work *less than 2 weeks* after giving birth (Bipartisan Policy Center, 2020a) due to lack of paid leave. Paid time off in both the lead-up to childbirth and in the weeks and months that follow is critical for a whole collection of reasons, not least of which is allowing mothers time to recover physically and receive postpartum medical care.

But the early weeks are also a critical time for bonding and attachment, to include (for many) the initiation of breastfeeding. Research suggests that paid family leave benefits support breastfeeding—with one study linking a 1-month increase in the duration of paid maternity leave with a 7.4 percentage point increase in the prevalence of breast-feeding initiation, a 5.9 percentage point increase in the prevalence of exclusive breastfeeding, and a 2.2-month increase in breastfeeding duration (Chai et al., 2018).

Why does that matter? In addition to being babies' best source of nutrition, breastfeeding has been linked by the Centers for Disease Control and Prevention (2023) to a host of positive long-term health outcomes, lowering the risk of everything from asthma, obesity, Type 1 diabetes, and sudden infant death syndrome (SIDS) to ear infections and stomach bugs. The American Academy of Pediatrics (2022) rec-ommends exclusive breastfeeding for the first 6 months of a child's life, to be continued alongside the introduction of solid foods up to the age of 2 or more.

Of course, breastfeeding and paid family leave aren't strictly linked . . . at least in theory. Is it possible to breastfeed without paid family leave? Sure. But is it likely? Absolutely not. And that should grab the attention of policymakers and taxpayers alike.

Take a moment to consider which members of the American work-force are least likely to access paid leave—and therefore breastfeed. Just who are these mothers forced to return to work within just 2 weeks after childbirth? And in what workplaces is breastfeeding more a pipe dream than a reality?

I'll give you a hint.

They are employees in the same low-income workplaces that lack paid health care benefits and retirement—leaving them to rely heavily on public income support programs, despite their full-time em-ployment (Center for the Study of Child Care Employment, 2021). Hourly staff in the fast-food industry, in big box stores, and—ironically enough—early childhood education.

Let that sink in for a moment. Infant-toddler teachers are, them-selves, so poorly compensated that they must often leave their own newborns, just days after delivery, to go care for those of others. (We'll discuss this more in the next chapter.)

When they do, they not only tend to forego breastfeeding practices that promise to reduce long-term health-care costs for their children, but put their own postpartum health at risk. And who covers the cost? The answer, in the simplest of terms, is all of us.

Still, breastfeeding is but one of many positive outcomes associated with paid parental leave. Knowing what you do from Chapter 1, you won't be surprised to learn that stable and nurturing parent-child re-lationships help to optimize early brain development.

Dr. Natalie Brito and colleagues (2022) have conducted fascinating research on the associations between paid parental leave and infant brain activity at 3 months of age. Using electroencephalography (EEG, a test that measures electrical activity in the brain) readings, the team's findings suggest that infants born to mothers accessing paid parental leave were more than seven times as likely to have mature patterns of brain activity compared to those of parents without such benefits.

Differences in early brain activity have also been recently reported among infants participating in an experimental trial of universal basic income for low-income mothers called Baby's First Years (Troller-Renfree et al., 2022). Again, using EEG readings, researchers found that children in families receiving $333 per month in universal basic income demonstrated greater activity in the test's high-frequency bands than did children in a control group receiving a stipend of only $20 per month. The results suggest that unconditional cash transfers to mothers experiencing poverty in the first year of their children's lives may actually change infant brain activity in ways associated with the development of cognitive skills.

In this case, it's not the cash that makes the difference. It's what the cash allows: time for infants and their mothers to bond and interact. It all comes back to *The Three Simple Truths*.

Fighting Crime and Protecting Our Nation

The potential for early childhood investment to reduce participants' interactions with the criminal justice system has been sprinkled throughout this chapter in association with the long-term savings generated to society. I won't dwell on the point here as a result but will take this opportunity to note that it's not just Heckman's fiscal analyses that include such findings.

The city of Chicago's publicly funded Child-Parent Centers have been providing preschool education and comprehensive family supports (spanning up to 6 years in total) to children from low-income families since 1967. A 2007 study of 1,539 participants (Reynolds et al., 2007) found that the program's preschool graduates had fewer felony arrests (16.5% vs. 21.1%) and lower rates of incarceration (20.6% vs. 25.6%) as compared to nonparticipants.

A study of Oklahoma's universal prekindergarten program (Smith, 2015) likewise documented diminished criminal activity, suggesting that participating preschoolers were 7% less likely to have been charged with a misdemeanor and 5% less likely to have been charged with a felony by age 19.

Again here, these benefits are not limited to classroom-based interventions. A 2010 analysis of the Nurse-Family Partnership program in Elmira, New York (Eckenrode et al., 2010), found that, relative to a matched comparison group, young mothers actively participating in the home-visiting program were less likely to have been arrested (10% vs. 30%) and/or convicted (4% vs. 20%) of crimes and had fewer lifetime arrests (mean: 0.10 vs. 0.54) and convictions (0.04 vs. 0.37) when tracked over time.

Putting aside the significant economic costs to taxpayers associated with incarceration, it is worth noting the qualitative benefits to society associated with diminished crime rates and improved public safety.

Speaking of safety, early childhood investments are increasingly linked to both the nation's global competitiveness and homeland security. But don't just take it from me; take it from Mike Petters, CEO of Huntington Ingalls Industries, the nation's largest builder of military ships. In a conversation with *The Business Journals* (McGinn & Posnanski, 2019), Petters put the matter succinctly:

> I don't just believe early childhood education is a national security issue. I believe it is THE national security issue.

Why, might you ask? Petters continues:

> In this century, with technology changing so much, if you want your children to be successful—and we all want our children to be successful—they will have to learn just about every day for the rest of their lives to keep up. Well, I can show you study after study that shows to make that happen, we need to instill a love of learning in them early, before school starts.

For Petters, investments in early childhood education will be key to ensuring not only the competitiveness of our military on the global stage, but the adequacy of its fighting force itself. In a keynote address at The Hunt Institute's 2019 Early Childhood Leadership Summit (Petters, 2019), the CEO noted that the talent pool from which the Pentagon has to choose is shrinking at an alarming rate—with as many as 4 in 5 young adults now unfit for military service due to failure to meet prerequisites associated with educational attainment, physical fitness, and/or a clean criminal record. As detailed throughout this chapter, all three are linked to investments in high-quality early child-hood education.

Promoting School Choice

Particularly in conservative political circles, school choice—the ability of parents to select the public or private education provider best suited to the needs of their child and family—is a popular educational reform. While bipartisan acceptance of the concept continues to grow, it is not without controversy, with opponents arguing that such choice holds the potential to undermine education writ large by diverting public dollars away from the nation's public schools.

Unlike K–12 education, which is primarily delivered via local school districts, the nation's early childhood landscape lacks a centralized structure and has long been dominated by choice—with preschool services delivered via "mixed delivery" systems, including a host of private, faith-, and community-based providers.

Because mixed delivery systems will be explored at length in Chapter 4, I will forego a more substantive discussion here and note, simply, that states' early childhood investments hold the potential to serve as laboratories for more broad-based versions of school choice.

Early Childhood Investment as a Moral Imperative

Finally, it's worth stating the obvious—a case that has been infused throughout this text since page 1: Investing in young children is a moral imperative.

Suppose for a moment that we had not just spent an entire chapter unpacking the economic, family strengthening, governmental, public safety, and national security benefits of public investment in kids. Suppose the data didn't make it the bipartisan slam dunk it so clearly is.

This chapter could have been a single sentence and still been compelling:

Investing in our most vulnerable is simply the right thing to do.

America's Payday Loan

Across these first two chapters, we have established both the critical importance of the early years and a compelling and wide-ranging bipartisan case for expanded public investment in the well-being of young children in accordance with *The Three Simple Truths*:

> (1) Learning begins in utero and never stops.
> (2) The period from prenatal to age 3 is a uniquely consequential window of human development during which the fundamental architecture of the brain is "wired."
> (3) Optimal brain development is dependent on stable, nurturing relationships with highly engaged adults.

The clearer this case becomes, the easier it is to see the folly of our current system—which might best be likened to mass reliance on a predatory payday loan. Because meeting our obligation to children would require potentially sharp increases in short-term spending, we continue to kick the can down the road, meeting our immediate obligations while willfully ignoring the *vastly increased* long-term costs of our inaction.

It's not by accident, incidentally, that this conversation has been framed around the concept of investment. The data suggest that is just what it will be—not a sunk cost, but a moneymaker. A developer of human capital. And a driver of state and federal prosperity.

The time for a paradigm shift—embraced by Democrats and Republicans alike—has arrived.

THE BIPARTISAN BLUEPRINT FOR CHANGE

Parents

Chapter 2 has focused on the bipartisan case for early childhood investment—and its contents hold practical implication for parents, both personally and politically.

On a personal level, the chapter provided a wealth of data on the long-term benefits associated with practices ranging from breastfeeding and paid family leave, to high-quality preschool and home visiting programs. As elsewhere, the keys to unlocking these benefits lie in both access and quality of implementation.

Want your child to benefit from the health, academic, financial, and life outcomes detailed in this chapter? I think we all do. But the reality is that our current system makes this easier said than done.

First, recognize that the programs/benefits discussed here are not available to all families. And when they are, they are rarely offered at the levels of quality, rigor, and intensity needed to replicate the results documented in the landmark studies cited here.

But *they could be.*

And that is where your knowledge and voice as a parent becomes so powerful.

What can you do to effect change in this space? Speak to the elected leaders by whom you are represented. Make sure that they, as leaders and key decision-makers, understand first and foremost that this is not only a bipartisan issue worthy of their support, but an investment in the future. (Note that Appendix B includes a detailed guide for policymaker outreach.)

And if that doesn't do the trick, go ahead and appeal to their more partisan instincts. Do you truly want a smaller government and di-minished tax burden? To strengthen the nuclear family? To increase school choice? Proactive investment in the years of early childhood is the way. In fact, it may be the only way. Let's dream of a world in which the greatest partisan divide on young children is not whether to act, but which party can dream bigger and act more boldly.

Professionals

Early childhood professionals need little convincing when it comes to the power of high-quality investments in young children. You see the benefits every day. Still, I hope that this chapter provided you with a concise set of talking points—and accompanying data—with which to help make the case on a bipartisan basis.

Like parents, you have an important role to play in helping to en-sure that policymakers see the big picture . . . as you do each day. One of the most powerful ways you can do so is to simply invite them to spend a couple of hours visiting your program. When they do, focus on a singular goal: uplifting all the ways that your educational envi-ronment and interactions with young children transcend basic care. Make your students' learning explicit, sharing what you do and why you do it. Help policymakers to understand that the roots of the com-petencies we hope to send high school graduates off into the world with begin in your classroom.

In fact, do so strategically. As I mentioned in the opening to this chapter, early childhood investment offers something for everyone. Take the time to learn about your policymakers' own stated priorities and help them make connections between what you're doing and what they're hoping to accomplish. The links are there, no matter who they might be.

Policymakers

Obviously, policymakers, this chapter was in large part for you. When it comes to the transformation of our public policy, you are the decision-makers with the power to change not only children's lives, but our state and national economies for the better.

There are multiple lessons in this chapter for you to act upon:

- *Start early.* Want to reap the long-term benefits and savings documented by Dr. Heckman and his peers? The key, as the Heckman Curve illustrates, is to start early—with the taxpayer dividends associated with programs beginning as early as 8 weeks nearly double those associated with prekindergarten alone.

- *Support parents as their children's first and best teachers.* When it comes to young children, our political discourse is prone to more than a little doublespeak. Policymakers routinely profess their desire to support the nuclear family and the benefits of stay-at-home parenting. But our policies— particularly as related to the needs of low-income families— often stray far from this ideal, setting strict work requirements that create distinct classes of parenthood, which may actually be exacerbating the challenges low-income students face as they enter the K–12 system.

  As we struggle to close the "achievement gap," consider that it may well be rooted in policies that send low-income mothers back to work within 2 weeks after delivery, often with low-quality or unstable care arrangements in place for their children during the most formative period of human development.

  Will the creation of new and expanded parental leave policies and early education benefits be costly? The answer is yes (at least in the short term). Is their absence even more costly? The answer is also yes.

- *Put your money where your mouth is.* If you take nothing else away from this chapter, it is my hope that it is the connection between early investment and your party's political platform—whichever platform that may be.

> » Small government?
> » Lower taxes?
> » Sustainability of the social safety net?
> » School choice?
> » Homeland security and public safety?
> » Improved health?
> » Strengthening families?
> » Supporting business and a thriving economy?

It's all in there. Use the information in this chapter to help make the case for the inclusion of high-quality early childhood investments as part of your campaigns, speeches, and state and federal party platforms.

CHAPTER 3

America's Failing Child Care Market

In this book's first chapter, I took pains to establish daycare—long misconceived as separate and distinct from education—as a fictional concept, a myth contradicted by decades of emerging brain science. Indeed, a core premise of this book is that the sooner we banish the terms *daycare* and *child care*, the sooner we will begin recognizing these settings for what they actually are for millions of American children: learning environments second only to the home in terms of their life-changing potential.

But this chapter is *about* child care—which, for better or worse, is the label commonly applied to the nation's private-sector early education programs (whether offered in center- or home-based settings). I'll revert to using the term here, *reluctantly and temporarily*, for two important reasons.

First, it's important to recognize that early childhood education lacks a centralized service delivery mechanism in the United States. Unlike K–12 education, which is largely delivered by public employees operating out of taxpayer-funded school buildings, programs serving the nation's youngest children are part of a vast and diverse public-private ecosystem. For this reason, the term *early childhood education* means different things to different people: Head Start, child care, publicly funded prekindergarten and kindergarten, home visiting programs . . . the list goes on and on.

As we unpack challenges to the sector, it's important to recognize that one segment—America's private child care market—finds itself in a particularly precarious spot, saddled by obstacles to success and solvency not necessarily shared by other programs in the space. For the sake of clarity, it is, therefore, important to distinguish between what is commonly referred to as child care and other programs falling under the early education umbrella.

The other reason I will use this label more liberally throughout this chapter is to spotlight exactly what the term has wrought. Child care is in a bad spot, in large part because of our persistent failure to see it as anything more than warehousing. The picture I have to paint isn't a pretty one. It is a portrait of a nation under the spell of the Daycare Myth.

That said, I want to make something crystal-clear at the outset. **What follows is an indictment of America's child care *policies and systems*, not the business owners and teachers they are failing.** As you'll find, America's child care professionals work under difficult conditions, with little respect, for unconscionable wages in the name of service to our children. They deserve better, and this book—harsh truths and all—is a heartfelt plea on their behalf.

CHILD CARE AS A BROKEN ECONOMIC MARKET

If you took an economics class in high school or college and remember anything at all, it is likely to be the laws of supply and demand, which generally govern the behaviors of the marketplace. Inextricably linked and in constant tension, supply and demand respond to each other in an endless dance. When a product or service is in high demand but supplies are low, prices can skyrocket. Sky-high prices rarely persist, however, due in part to the motivation they provide to competing entrepreneurs to get in on the profits. As supply increases, both price and demand tend to decrease, helping most markets to settle back into a healthy equilibrium, at least for a time. And around and around it goes.

That said, you might have noticed that I used some important qualifiers in those last couple sentences—words like "generally," "tend to," and "most." That's because, in almost all things, there are exceptions to the rules. And when it comes to economics, child care is one such exception. It is a *broken market*—a situation in which the textbook laws of supply and demand don't always apply. There are multiple reasons for the market's dysfunction, and we'll explore each in depth over the coming pages.

Chief among them, as I'll continue to outline in this chapter, is a fundamental mismatch between what parents, policymakers, and even some providers *believe the market exists to provide* (care) and *what it actually does provide* (brain building), however suboptimally in the current climate. Resolving this mismatch is a public policy imperative at both the state and federal levels. When it comes to child care, it's often as if we're having a discussion about how best to run a hot dog stand when the real product is fine dining. There may be some outward similarities, but our business assumptions are *wildly* off base.

To illustrate this point, let's play a game.

Pretend, for just a moment, that you are an entrepreneur planning to enter the child care space—a prospective business owner with all the right intentions but limited knowledge of (or, perhaps, interest in) *The Three Simple Truths*. As you ponder a hypothetical business plan, consider how powerfully your understanding of your *product* might serve to shape your cost assumptions and operations. I'll play along.

Let's start with the fundamental question: *Just what am I in the business of selling?*

If the answer is primarily supervision and safety, my imaginary business plan would aim to deliver both in spades—maximizing enrollment and profit by providing enough of both—but also *just enough* low-wage, adult caretakers to ensure that children are happy, warm, safe, and well-nourished during their time in my care. I don't say any of this disparagingly, incidentally. Think of it like a really decent summer camp.

Now overlay *The Three Simple Truths* (learning begins in utero and never stops; the period from prenatal to age 3 is a uniquely consequential window of human development during which the fundamental architecture of the brain is "wired"; and optimal brain development is dependent on stable, nurturing relationships with highly engaged adults) and reconsider your response.

What if your business provided—but was no longer premised upon—the concept of care? Suppose your product was now something else entirely: the optimization of human potential and co-creation of brain architecture. How might your business model change if it was intended, at its very core, to shepherd children onto a path of lifelong success?

I can tell you one thing: *Mine would look nothing like the first example.* Aside from some superficial commonalities, we'd be talking about an entirely different ballgame.

For starters, I'd need to reconsider enrollment capacity. There's an enormous difference between "How many kids can I keep safe and well-nourished for 8 hours?" and "How might I best optimize the early brain development of *every child* enrolled?" I would need to serve fewer kids . . . likely many fewer.

I'd also need to revisit my staffing assumptions. Not only would I require lower student-teacher ratios, but I would need just that: *teachers*. Delivery of this product would require well-trained and commensurately compensated child development experts—adults prepared not only to supervise children's safety and well-being but also to engage with them deeply and planfully.

As for that whole maximizing profits piece? I might as well kiss that idea goodbye. We'd be talking about a far more costly service. I might be able to provide it profitably to the ultra-wealthy, but almost certainly not at scale.

Herein lies the challenge. When it comes to child care, we're operating on all the wrong assumptions. It's not just that our solutions are ineffective—it's that we're not even directing them at the right problems. And yet, despite the low bar we've set for it, our current child care model simply doesn't work.

And it doesn't because it *can't*.

Child Care's Three-Legged Stool

Let's talk for just a moment about the economics of child care—not the aspirational version I'll continue to outline, but the care-based model just as it is now. The major problem with child care—and the fundamental reason behind its broken market status—is that it is a product (1) required by millions that is (2) more expensive to provide than almost any individual consumer can afford.

Why is it so expensive? First, child care has high and inescapable overhead costs. Unlike small businesses that can be run with a laptop computer out of a spare bedroom or coffee shop, child care requires classroom space, and—in the case of center-based programs—a sizable amount of it. Add state regulations that may necessitate significant upfitting of this space to meet local fire codes, enable food preparation, and ensure general safety, and you're looking at substantial costs even before the first child sets foot in the program.

Second, child care is fundamentally labor-intensive, requiring real live humans to staff each classroom. Despite the wonders of technology, we're yet to automate the feeding of a hungry baby or the changing of a dirty diaper, much less the education of our young children. What's more, even when premised on basic health and safety, there remain both legal and practical limits to the number of children served in each classroom.

Sure, larger programs may find certain economies of scale when it comes to bulk purchasing and back-office business operations like billing and payroll processing, but there's little way around the fact that—as a front-line service—child care boils down to adults, children, and classroom space. None of these costs are easily minimized. And in many cases, they can't *legally* be minimized any more than they already are.

Economists have a special name for services that benefit society but are too costly for individual consumers. They call them *public goods*. As citizens, we aren't generally left to our own devices when it comes to the provision of roads and schools. Except in rural areas, we don't often create our own water and sewer systems or our own electrical grids. Instead, the cost-effective provision of this infrastructure—which benefits us all—is generally the role of government.

In the United States, *education* is widely acknowledged as public good. *Care*, at least currently, is not, leaving every family to fend for itself. If this sets off your "Daycare Myth Detector," it should. By failing to recognize child care as a form of education, we persist in expecting its cost to be shouldered by individual consumers.

The results have been nothing short of disastrous. Left to the whims of a broken market, child care is a wobbly three-legged stool (Figure 3.1), (barely) propped up by providers, parents, and the early childhood workforce—and providing all the quality you'd expect of such a system. Over the coming pages we'll look at the unique role and challenges faced by each of these stakeholder groups.

Child Care as a Calling

Looking to start a business? Here's an important word of advice: Child care is not a get-rich-quick scheme. In fact, if your goal is to make money, you could hardly choose a less promising field. Child care businesses operate on razor-thin margins, with staffing costs ranging from

Figure 3.1. Child Care as a Three-Legged Stool

60% to 80% and typical profits—even in rosier times—averaging less than 1% (Grunewald & Davies, 2011). Indeed, the very notion of "for profit" child care is, for most businesses, a bit of a misnomer. They may not enjoy the tax benefits of nonprofit status, but believe me, nonprofit they are.

As most readers know painfully well, recent years have presented unique challenges for the industry, with the COVID-19 pandemic only exacerbating an already precarious business model. Nearly 16,000 American child care providers closed their doors for good during the pandemic (Child Care Aware of America, 2022), with thousands of others remaining solvent only by virtue of temporary COVID relief dollars appropriated by Congress. As other industries strive to maximize profits, child care businesses routinely struggle just to keep their doors open.

It begs the question: Why start a child care business at all? If the field is hard and (at best) minimally profitable, why bother? As it turns out, the question of *why* is often inextricably linked to the question of *who*.

So, just who does own these businesses?

The answer, overwhelmingly, is women. According to the National Women's Business Council (2020), 96.5% of child care businesses are women-owned, employing a workforce that is, itself, 94% female. Roughly half of these businesses are minority-owned, giving women of color a sizable (if not majority) ownership stake in the field.

What's more, child care puts the *small* in small business. In 2018, a reported 88% of all child care businesses were solo practitioners, operating out of their homes, employing no one else but themselves (U.S. Census Bureau, 2020), and generating revenue of around $16,000 per year (Boushey et al., 2022). If that dollar figure seems astonishingly low, that's because it is. As small business owners, family child care providers have the flexibility to charge below-market rates, often generating personal income that equates to less than minimum wage for the services they render.

As for the question of *why*, the answers range from altruism to necessity to (strangely enough) the lack thereof. For many, child care is simply a calling. Putting aside for a moment the handful of national child care chains (whose operations are premised on a whole different set of assumptions and whose role we'll discuss in the next chapter), you'll find that the overwhelming majority of child care businesses—whether home- or center-based—are labors of love, small family businesses run by adults with a greater passion for helping families and children than for self-benefit.

Take Wisconsin family child care owner Corrine Hendrickson, for example, who recently explained to Boston-area National Public Radio affiliate WBUR that, prior to the receipt of federal COVID relief dollars, she was paying herself only $6 an hour—some 18% less than the federal minimum wage of $7.25. The reason, according to Hendrickson? Paying herself any more would require her to raise rates on struggling families. Break-even businesses like Hendrickson's are routinely enabled by dual-income households in which the child care provider contributes but is not expected to sustain her family single-handedly (Sutherland & Chakrabarti, 2023).

In some cases, child care businesses originate from a caregiving need of the provider's own. Wanting—or needing—to care for one's own child(ren), the option of taking on additional children (at even a modest fee) may help to offset otherwise lost wages. This same motivation drives teachers in many center-based programs, who accept employment through which they can remain connected with their own child throughout the day in exchange for free or reduced-price tuition.

This same spirit of altruism often holds true for the operators of small center-based programs, who may be driven more by a calling to service than by ruthless profit motive. It's worth noting here that altruism and business sense needn't be mutually exclusive . . . though they sometimes seem to be in the child care market. Owner-operators entering the field with more love for children than business management experience are often further disadvantaged. In Chapter 5 we'll talk about steps being taken by states to promote strong business practices, including business coaching and incubator programs designed to help providers maximize limited resources. These programs will never overcome child care's fundamental economic challenge but can at least help staunch some of the bleeding.

If this all leaves you (reasonably) wondering, "So, why not just charge more?" the answer comes down to this: Even at current rates . . . even at current levels of quality . . . child care is bleeding parents dry.

The Customer Isn't King: Unpacking the Role of Parents

Perhaps you've heard the expression, "The customer is king?" In the free market, entrepreneurs create magic when they are able to (1) cater to the precise needs of their customers, (2) deliver the products and services they desire, and (3) charge customers at price points that make their consumption not only possible, but robust. If you need any further evidence of child care's broken market status, try overlaying the experience of parents against the description above. You're likely to find that the nation's child care system is failing parents on all three counts.

Does child care cater to the needs of parents? The answer is—at best—a qualified *sometimes.* If you work a 9-to-5, white-collar job every Monday through Friday you may be in luck, as most child-care businesses maintain operating hours consistent with your work schedule. But suppose you work evenings, or overnights? Maybe your schedule varies from week to week, as is common in retail. Perhaps you need care on the weekends? Well, good luck with that.

Does child care deliver the products and services parents desire? In other words, does it deliver what *their children need to thrive?* For reasons we'll get into as we discuss the early childhood workforce, the answer here is almost a universal *no*, though parents (for the sake of their own mental health) may be loath to admit it, even to themselves.

And is it delivered at a comfortable price point? (I'll pause here for just a moment to allow your laughter to subside.) As child care consumers, parents aren't monarchs. A more realistic expression could be: "You'll take what you get, if you're lucky enough to get it at all, and you'll pay more than you ever imagined for the privilege."

It's not uncommon for expectant couples—often spurred to action by their own parents—to open college savings accounts. After all, the expenses associated with higher education can be so massive that even 17 years is, for many Americans, an insufficient timeline over which to prepare.

What few recognize is that childbirth comes accompanied by a similar and far more immediate cost. Whether realized in the form of child care tuition or as an opportunity cost (in the form of lost or foregone wages associated with one or both parents' election to oversee caregiving responsibilities themselves), the price of parenthood can be staggering.

According to one recent analysis (Patel, 2023), child care is now more expensive than in-state college tuition at public universities in 28 states, costing an average of $1,031 more per year than higher education. In 2020, home lender Freddie Mac (Khater et al., 2020) likewise reported that monthly child care expenses amount to roughly half of the nation's median mortgage payment and 80% of its median rent, placing a strain on families in both directions and limiting their options in the housing market.

How might we assess the rate at which child care might be considered "affordable" for families? The most commonly cited definition, established by the U.S. Department of Health and Human Services in 2016, is 7% of a family's annual household income—though it is important to recognize that this figure was intended to set a ceiling for co-payment rates among low-income families receiving child care subsidies and not as a general measure of affordability (Smith et al., 2020). That said, 7% remains the de facto standard, so let's look at how child care costs compare to this benchmark in states across the nation.

As illustrated in Figure 3.2 (Patel, 2023), not a single state meets this affordability standard, with child care in Utah ranked as the nation's most budget-friendly at a cost equivalent to 7.87% of the state's annual mean salary. A careful look at the data, however, reveals that

Figure 3.2. The Affordability of Child Care in Every U.S. State (Patel, 2023)

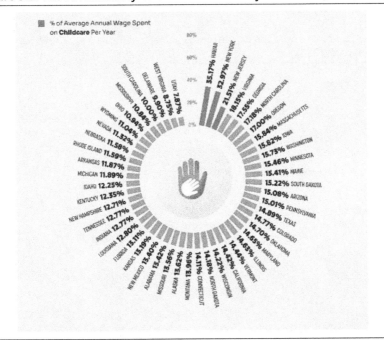

Source: NetCredit, https://www.netcredit.com/blog/cost-of-child-care-by-state/#:~ :text=Hawaii%20and%20New%20York%20are,terms%20(%2423%2C231%20 per%20year)

Utah is something of an outlier, with parents in 47 states paying more than 10% of their annual wage, fully half the nation (25 states) paying 14% or more (twice the affordability standard), and parents in New York and Hawaii saddled with child care costs equivalent to roughly one-third of the state's median income.

At rates like this, it's easy to understand why child care has become a major predictor of workforce participation . . . or in this case, the lack thereof. Faced with the reality that—after taxes and child care costs—work is suddenly far less lucrative (and in some cases a virtual wash), many parents (and mothers in particular) make the decision to leave the workforce altogether. Compare the data in Figure 3.3 and Figure 3.4, in which the Federal Reserve Bank of St. Louis (Gascon, 2023) compares the recent labor force participation rates of native-born American men and women.

The differences are stark. When it comes to the parents of children under the age of 3, the labor force participation of fathers is at its very highest (at roughly 95%), while the employment of mothers not only lags by more than 25% but is also at its lowest when compared to other phases of parenthood.

Figure 3.3. Labor Force Participation Rate, Native-Born Men, 2005–2022 (Gascon, 2023)

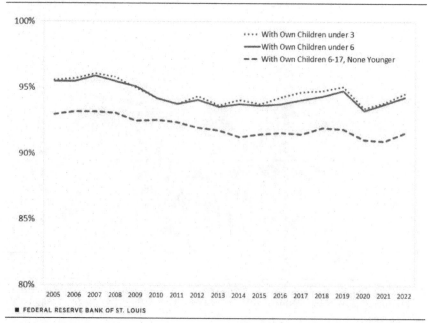

Figure 3.4. Labor Force Participation Rate, Native-Born Women, 2005–2022 (Gascon, 2023)

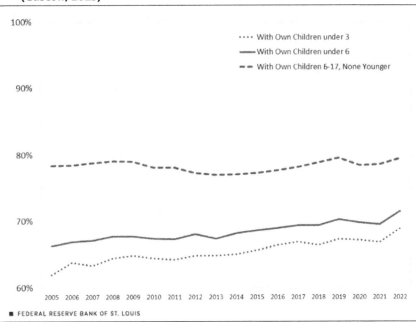

■ FEDERAL RESERVE BANK OF ST. LOUIS

There are different ways of looking at this data, of course. In at least some cases, this is a deliberate, tactical choice on the part of families, consistent with *The Three Simple Truths,* an acknowledgment that—for these families—a parent is best equipped to maximize their child's early years. For others, the choice is one made by necessity and may be accompanied by great economic hardship.

In either case, the election to withdraw from the workforce, for even a period of just a few years, is one with long-term financial implications. According to one analysis (Budig, 2014), mothers see their long-term earnings potential drop by 4% for each child they have. This "motherhood penalty," the result of time away from the workforce during which women forego both wages and opportunities for advancement, may also limit opportunity for those seeking to reenter the workforce, with data suggesting mothers seeking new employment after a family-related break in service are only half as likely to land job interviews as mothers laid off by their previous employers (Weisshaar, 2018).

From a policy perspective, the real challenge here extends beyond making child care less expensive; it speaks to the need to better support the choices of American parents, honoring and enabling the decisions of those who elect to educate and care for their children at home, while making high-quality early childhood education affordable and readily accessible for those electing (or required) to work outside the home.

In reality, child care is neither affordable nor accessible for a majority of American families. That's because in addition to its devastating costs, for many, it is virtually impossible to find.

An analysis by the Center for American Progress (2018) finds that 51% of American families reside in a child care desert, which they define as "any census tract with more than 50 children under age 5 that contains either no child care providers or so few options that there are more than three times as many children as licensed child care slots." When you think of a child care desert, you might first be tempted to envision a literal desert—rural areas in which few businesses of any kind manage to flourish. And that's definitely one contributor to the phenomenon. Rural America and low-income neighborhoods are certainly lacking in child care. But it might surprise you to know that many of the nation's most high-income communities are also deserts.

According to the Center's data, 43% of families in the nation's highest-income neighborhoods find themselves situated in child care deserts (compared with 54% of families in the lowest-income neighborhoods). Indeed, child care's broken economic model presents just as many—if not more—challenges in high-income communities (where both commercial real estate costs and elevated costs of living conspire against the success of child care businesses). The bottom line is this: Whether you reside in an urban, rural, or suburban area, child care in this country is every bit as inaccessible as it is expensive, routinely leaving parents in the position of settling not for the best, but for the best they can find and afford.

Low-Income Women of Color Help Subsidize the Cost of Child Care

When it comes to the sale of goods and services in the free market, we typically think of transactions as a two-way proposition between producers and consumers. But that's not always the way things work. In some industries, there's a third participant: government.

It's not a topic that always gets the attention it deserves, but a whole host of industries—from agriculture, automotive manufacturing, banking, and airlines, to oil and energy—benefit from your tax dollars. The rationale is not dissimilar from our discussion of public goods earlier. While perhaps not fully supported in the style of roads and public schools, these private industries are so critical to the success of the overall economy that, in practice, they're deemed *too big to fail*. And so, when U.S. automakers or banks encounter financial peril, it's a safe bet the government will intervene. Often this is done proactively in the form of subsidies.

Agriculture, where the federal government invests a whopping $30 billion a year, is a prime example. In the United States, we subsidize virtually all aspects of agriculture, protecting farmers from variations in prices and revenue, and subsidizing the costs of crop insurance, land, loans, marketing, and more (Edwards, 2023).

What's more, the federal government subsidizes specific crops, influencing not only their cost, but ultimately what we eat. Remember the base of the 1992 Food Pyramid we discussed in Chapter 1? The one that recommended 6–11 servings of bread, cereal, rice, and pasta daily? Would it surprise you to know that the nation's most heavily subsidized crops (corn, soy, wheat, and rice) align almost perfectly with the federal government's dubious nutritional advice (Hayes & Kerska, 2021)?

I'll leave that particular mystery for another author to explore. For now, my point is simply that the costs of goods and services in this country aren't always what they seem and are often made more affordable (in the checkout line, if not on your tax return) by hidden players who help to underwrite their cost.

Believe it or not, such is also the case with child care. But, for most consumers, it's not the government lurking in the shadows to make tuition more affordable—it's the low-income women who comprise the nation's early childhood workforce.

That's right; low-income women—many of them women of color—are helping to subsidize *your* child care bill in the form of their unconscionably low wages.

Addressing Sexism, Classism, and Racism in America's Child Care Systems

Have you ever squeezed a balloon? If so, you know that as you apply pressure to one area, the displaced air will cause another part to bulge outward—exerting still greater pressure on the newly formed bubble. Child care's three-legged stool works in much the same fashion, with the squeeze applied in a most unfortunate way.

Struggling to make ends meet and keep their doors open, program operators scrape by on the narrowest of margins. Parents pay more than they reasonably can just for the privilege of a slot. And the whole sad affair gets hefted on the backs of the child care workforce, who earn—in most cases—at or near their states' minimum wage just to make the books balance.

According to the U.S. Bureau of Labor Statistics (2022), America's child care teachers earn a median wage of $13.71 an hour, some 59 cents less than animal caretakers such as dog walkers. And with a pandemic-constrained workforce rapidly driving up the wages of fast food workers (McCarthy, 2023) and other traditionally low-wage employees (DiPalma, 2023), it's not impossible to think that the child care workforce may soon find itself holding the dubious distinction as America's most poorly paid.

Not surprisingly, the field's astonishingly low wages have a direct correlation with the duration of teachers' employment, with some estimates suggesting up to 40% annual turnover in these roles (Tate Sullivan, 2021). At precisely the time that developmental science tells us children most require stable, nurturing relationships, our child care system provides them with the opposite: a revolving door of temporary caregivers.

How did we get here? With the brain science clear and the academic, economic, and lifelong benefits of high-quality early childhood education so thoroughly documented, how is it that we as a society find it acceptable that those who hand French fries through a window earn more than those responsible for the literal co-construction of our young children's brains?

The answer has everything to do with sexism, classism, and racism. Indeed, this nation's women—and women of color, in particular—have a long history of caring for the children of others, not as a (well-deserved) position of honor, but as a menial task beneath those of wealth and privilege. Indeed, it was once commonplace in the Deep South for enslaved Black women to care for, and even breastfeed, the white children of their masters—a tradition that continued long after the Civil War through the unpaid or underpaid service of Black domestic servants (Goss-Graves, 2021).

More than 160 years after the signing of the Emancipation Proclamation, our vision of child care as menial work continues to undergird the Daycare Myth, with the women of the child care workforce lagging far behind even their peers in other early childhood settings (kindergarten classrooms, Head Start programs, etc.). Two indicators, in particular, help to tell the tale of their economic hardship.

According to a study from the Center for the Study of Child Care Employment at the University of California, Berkeley (2021), child care teachers earn a "living wage" (sufficient to cover their basic needs for food and shelter given the local cost of living) in only 10 states: Alaska, Arizona, Colorado, Maine, Minnesota, Nebraska, North Dakota, Vermont, Washington, and Wyoming. Bear in mind that this analysis is premised on a household of *one*. The wages of child care professionals with one or more children do not currently meet the living wage standard *in any state.*

Not surprisingly, given both their low incomes and the widespread absence of employer-provided health care benefits in the field, the child care workforce relies heavily on safety-net programs such as Medicaid, the Children's Health Insurance Program, and Supplemental Nutrition Assistance Program (food stamps), with a reported 53% forced to tap public benefits (First Five Years Fund, 2022). These aren't the unemployed "welfare queens" of political stereotype. These are women who are employed in critical, full-time jobs whose wages nonetheless qualify them for public assistance.

And in doing so—by acquiescing to wages that are both inequitable and far out of step with their importance to society—the women of America's child care workforce subsidize the price of care for us all: rich, poor, and everywhere in between.

I'll drive the point home with one last story.

I recently had the chance to spend a week supporting a midwestern state as part of a stakeholder listening tour on its early childhood system. In school cafeterias and at community nonprofit organizations across the state, I had the opportunity to facilitate conversation with policymakers, parents, and early childhood leaders to hear how things were going for young children, their families, and the professionals who meet their needs each day. One child care owner stood out among all the rest.

Asked about her needs and how the state might best support her program, she paused thoughtfully, and suggested that her greatest need was a floating substitute teacher capable of rotating from classroom to classroom to provide relief for the staff assigned to each. Such positions exist in many schools, so the suggestion didn't initially take me by surprise.

"Oh, that's a great idea," I responded. "You mean someone who would cover lunch breaks and bathroom trips for the teachers?"

"Well, not really that," she explained. "We mostly have that covered. My problem is that I need to schedule coverage each week so everyone can get to the bank. It's only open a few hours a week."

In this age of direct deposit, I became a little confused. Why were they leaving work to visit a bank?

"To deposit their checks?" I asked.

"No, no . . . not that kind of a bank. I try to provide time each week for my teachers to visit our local food bank. What I can pay them really isn't enough to feed their families."

We should all be ashamed.

Government Subsidies and the Illusion of Support

As referenced briefly in this chapter, the federal government does supply some level of child care support to low-income working families. Through the Child Care and Development Block Grant (CCDBG), states receive funding to provide child care subsidies tied to work and continuing education, typically accompanied by a health insurance-style *co-payment* requiring families to pay a proportional share linked to income.

Under federal rules, the receipt of these subsidies is currently limited to families earning no more than 85% of state median income. This threshold varies by state, currently ranging from $51,883 in Mississippi (home of the nation's lowest median income) to $124,474 in the District of Columbia (the nation's highest) for a two-person household (U.S. Department of Justice, 2023). But states are permitted to enact more stringent guidelines and, perhaps wisely, do, given the insufficiency of federal funding for the program. How far off from their own definition is Congress?

According to a recent analysis by the U.S. Government Accountability Office (GAO) depicted in Figure 3.5, some 13.5 million children met the federal eligibility requirements for subsidized care in 2017. With the limited funding appropriated by Congress, however, only 1 in 7 of those children (1.9 million or 14%) actually *received* support. In short, while the program may be a godsend for those who receive it, it is an empty promise for 11.6 million American families eligible under the federal government's own definition of need.

What's worse, federal guidelines governing the program may be actively exacerbating the industry's precarious financial state. We'll explore that question in greater depth in the next chapter.

Figure 3.5. CCDBG Eligibility vs. Receipt (U.S. Government Accountability Office, 2021)

Health and Human Services' Estimated Number of Children Eligible Under Federal and State Rules, and Estimated Number Receiving Child Care Subsidies, Fiscal Year 2017

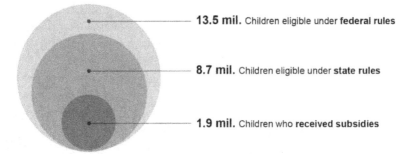

13.5 mil. Children eligible under **federal rules**

8.7 mil. Children eligible under **state rules**

1.9 mil. Children who **received subsidies**

Source: Office of the Assistant Secretary for Planning and Evaluation, U.S. Department of Health and Human Services, *Factsheet: Estimates of Child Care Eligibility and Receipt for Fiscal Year 2017* (Washington, D.C.: November 2020). | GAO-21-245R

Training and Credentialing

Finally, let's take a look at the qualifications of America's child care workforce. As we do, bear in mind that we're talking about the workforce writ large and *not* individual teachers, many of whom far exceed the minimal expectations set by states and programs. Indeed, it is these teachers (if you're taking the time to read this book, I'm almost certainly talking about you) whom we should aspire to have staffing all of America's classrooms.

At the beginning of this chapter, I explained why it would be important for me to distinguish child care from other forms of early childhood education, noting that pay and credentialing often look quite different across settings. Public school prekindergarten teachers, for example, are almost always public employees holding bachelor's degrees or higher as well as state certification, and earning the same salary and benefits offered to elementary school teachers. Lead teachers in federally funded Head Start classrooms—though not always public employees or compensated at quite the same level as public school employees—are required to hold 2- or 4-year degrees in early childhood education (with at least 50% of a program's lead teachers required to hold a 4-year-degree).

As a general rule of thumb, the bar for becoming a child care teacher is far lower, requiring only a high school diploma or its equivalent and a small number of annual training hours in most states—though this threshold is, for many, just a starting point. Requirements vary by geography, but many state quality-rating systems and national accrediting bodies (including the National Association for the Education of Young Children, commonly acknowledged as the field's "gold standard") require more advanced credentialing and typically command higher payment rates, both from parents and state subsidy systems as a result.

While few would argue against the need for a well-qualified workforce, the practical realities described throughout this chapter and outdated public perceptions associated with the Daycare Myth conspire against advanced education/training.

I mean, let's get real: Imagine requiring someone to pursue an advanced degree while paying them less—and in a growing number of cases, *considerably less*—than they could make as a starting cashier at McDonald's or Walmart. Our broken child care system simply isn't aligned with such credentialing, nor, in many cases, is higher education even a perceived need.

Truth be told, even if money and time were not objects, the nation's 4-year college systems aren't currently equipped to meet the needs of child care professionals. If you have a 4-year degree in early childhood education, chances are that you've been prepared to teach in the primary grades rather than an infant-toddler classroom. Colleges cater to the demands of their students. And no one is clamoring to take out $50,000 in student loans in exchange for a job that pays $10 an hour.

The nation's 2-year technical and community colleges provide a vastly superior product to this market, often in partnership with state agencies overseeing the Child Care and Development Block Grant. Recognizing the challenges associated with balancing (often grueling) full-time work and continuing education, many states have created "stackable" credentials (Daugherty et al., 2023) in which teachers complete topical modules that combine over time into state-issued credentials and eventually associate degrees. Completion of this coursework is often free of charge to participating teachers and/or accompanied by a small stipend or raise upon completion. *But with upward of 40% of teachers leaving the workforce each year, a sizable portion of this investment vanishes, annually, into thin air.* We'll look at some promising (and not-so-promising) solutions in the coming chapters.

As I close this chapter, I want to echo a sentiment introduced in this book's opening pages: In need of affordable, high-quality early childhood education provided by well-trained, expert adults, America's children and families are being failed by its systems on each and every count. Indeed, it is as if we have created a bizarro world in which up is down, day is night, and everything children need to thrive is being systematically withheld.

It's time for us to sound the alarm and make some changes.

THE BIPARTISAN BLUEPRINT FOR CHANGE

Parents

As the parent of a young child, I suspect that this chapter was as difficult for you to read as it was for me to write. The truth is that our child care policies and systems are in a state of terrible disrepair. This has obvious implications for your family and for all of those you love. My advice to you here is twofold—pertaining first to the care of your own child and then to our systems more broadly.

Finding the right program for your child. First, just as I was careful to note that this chapter's description of child care teacher credentials was applicable to the system—*but not necessarily to individual teachers*—I want to offer the reassurance that there are terrific programs out there, programs that manage, against all odds, to deliver a consistently high-quality product despite the challenging environment in which they are forced to operate. The trick is finding them. And I'm going to teach you how. (This isn't a systemic solution to the problems we've discussed, but it is guidance you'll benefit from right here and now.)

At the end of Chapter 1, I advised you to carve out time to visit prospective early education programs and to watch closely for the quality of their adult-child interactions. Remember that nothing is more important than attentive and nurturing teachers and that these are the adults who will co-construct your child's brain.

For these reasons it's not enough to find a single teacher who impresses you. What you want is a program built around—and populated, day in and day out—by amazing adults.

Here I'd like to share some additional guidance on how to determine whether the program itself is conducive to their hiring and retention. Doing so will require a short interview with the program director. This may strike you as a little pushy, and that's okay. When it comes to your child, be a little pushy. It's a skill that will serve you both well.

Here are a few key questions to consider asking the program director, along with a brief explanation of why each matters and what you should be hoping to hear:

- What is your starting pay for a lead teacher? Does this vary according to credentials?
  Recognize that this figure is unlikely to knock your socks off . . . and is probably not going to be significantly higher than your state's minimum wage. But it matters, nonetheless. A starting wage at the state's legal minimum is a red flag for likely teacher attrition. Look for a rate that makes the program competitive in the market and for teachers holding advanced credentials to be compensated at higher rates.
- Do your teachers have employer-paid health care and/or retirement benefits?
  In many cases, sadly, the answer to this question is going to be no. As the industry standard, particularly in non-unionized states, this isn't necessarily a deal-breaker—but consider it a very positive sign if the answer is yes. This is a program that is working actively to support and retain its employees.
- Do your teachers have paid sick leave?
  Pay careful attention to this response. If the answer is no, this is a program in which your child's teacher may be forced to report to work even when ill/contagious, a sign that neither your child's well-being nor the teacher's is the program's top priority.
- What education or credentialing do you require for teachers?
  Ideally, you'll looking for something more than a high school diploma or GED here, especially in the case of lead teachers. Look for some evidence of advanced degrees, or—at minimum—a credential like the Child Development Associate (CDA), which requires 120 clock hours of early childhood training.
- What sort of annual training do you provide for teachers?
  The point here is not necessarily to get into the details of the specific training provided, but instead to establish whether ongoing professional development is a part of the program's culture. Do teachers receive paid time off to attend professional conferences, for example, or are they required to identify and cover the costs of their own state-mandated training? Does the program make any accommodations for staff enrolling in higher education coursework?

- How long has your longest-serving teacher been employed by the program? What is the average length of employment for a lead teacher?
  This might be the single most important question you ask.
  Particularly in a high-turnover field like child care, programs that retain key staff over a period of years tend to be well-run and staffed by happy teachers.
- Has the state assigned your program a quality rating? If so, what is it?
  Most but not all states have a tiered quality rating system designed to help parents identify programs of high quality. This may entail the assignment of letter grades like a report card or star ratings. Know that a state's highest rating is often quite difficult and costly to obtain. It's certainly a good sign to find a program at the top. Perhaps more importantly, exercise caution around programs at or near the bottom of this scale. Take a few minutes to research your state's system in advance of your visit. Better yet, many state agencies administering child care programs have searchable websites through which you can identify program ratings in advance—which may be a great way to help narrow your search from the get-go.
- Is your program accredited by the National Association for the Education of Young Children (NAEYC) or the National Association for Family Child Care (NAFCC)?
  Extending beyond most state rating systems are national accreditations issued by external bodies like NAEYC and NAFCC. These accreditations require a serious commitment of time and resources to attain and are an excellent indicator of quality. It's not necessarily a red flag to discover that a program isn't nationally accredited (relatively few are), but consider it a waving green flag if they are.
- In addition to parent tuition payments, does the center have other sources of support or revenue?
  Finally, this question is an important indicator of the program's likely fiscal stability. Does the program accept state subsidies for low-income children who might not otherwise be able to enroll? Does it receive partial funding (including the provision of classroom space or utilities) from a federal grant or an associated church, business, school district, hospital, or philanthropy? The more diverse a program's revenue, the greater the likelihood that its teachers are well-compensated, stably employed, and happy.

None of these questions are intended to be high-stakes in and of themselves but, taken in combination, should provide you a far more detailed portrait of the program than a simple walk-through might otherwise provide. When you find a program with adult/child interactions that inspire your confidence and is capable of putting its best foot forward on most of the questions above, you've likely found a winner.

Making your voice heard. Armed with a reasonably solid plan to find the right program for your child, there's one more step I'd ask you to consider: share your story. Tell your friends, tell your family, and tell your policymakers about your experience. Tell them about the sacrifices you're having to make. Tell them how your child care cost stacks up against your mortgage or rent and what you're unable to do as a result. Most importantly, share the stories of the programs that you've visited—what you've learned about the wages and benefits of those charged with nurturing our most treasured resource. Let them know that henceforth you will be a *child care voter*, measuring their success (in part) on their support of children, families, and taxpayers as related to the provision of accessible and affordable early childhood education in your community.

Professionals

Can I share a confession? More than any other section of this book, this is the one I agonized over the longest. Staring endlessly at a blank page and a flashing cursor, I puzzled over what advice I might possibly offer child care professionals after enumerating the fundamental inequities and brokenness of the system in which you toil daily on behalf of children and families. To make it all right. To help it make sense. Here's the best I've got.

We are rapidly approaching a tipping point after which the American public will never look at your work in the same way. It is my hope that this book will help to hasten a reckoning with the Daycare Myth and that the respect and compensation you so richly deserve are on the way.

You are a critical part of the solution. So, pull no punches. And speak your truth to anyone and everyone who will listen. Help parents to understand the challenges you face. Reach out to policymakers to share the urgency of your situation. Be advocates for change. But then do what's right for you.

In his book *Atomic Habits*, author James Clear (2018) set forth an idea that continues to hit me like a gut punch:

You do not rise to the level of your goals. You fall to the level of your systems.

Clear was speaking of the power of personal habits in helping us reach our goals. But I think the same holds true for those struggling within child care's own deeply flawed system. Undoing a hundred-plus years of ill-conceived public policy and poorly informed public perception is a big hill to climb—and a task that isn't within your personal wherewithal. It's something that will take a groundswell and perhaps a crisis of such proportion that policymakers are forced to act. I believe we're approaching critical mass on both fronts.

Until then, we will continue falling to the level of our systems, which is why early childhood systems reform must be America's most pressing domestic public policy priority.

What does this mean for you personally? It's a question only you can answer. But here's what I'll tell you: It's not your responsibility to make other people's child care marginally affordable at the cost of feeding your own family. And it's deeply wrong that your critical work is valued less than that of so many others. I hope you'll stay. So many children and families are blessed by your commitment and passion. But I understand why our field experiences such astronomical levels of turnover.

If child care isn't the place for you, if only because you're finding it impossible to make ends meet, I understand. If that's the case, I urge you to move on from the work, but never from the fight.

Either way, thank you. Thank you. Thank you.

Policymakers

If I haven't said it clearly up to this point, let me be clear: *Policymakers, this book is for you.* The reason for this, of course, is that you—and ultimately you alone—have the wherewithal to reenvision America's public policy when it comes to young children and their families.

Yes, child care needs your attention urgently. But this is about more than just child care. As we've established throughout this book, it's about families and children, it's about employers, and it's about taxpayers—even those without a single child of their own.

Across the remainder of this book, I'll turn to discussion of public policy solutions and pitfalls for you to explore and avoid, spotlighting

innovative (and a handful of not-so-innovative) solutions from across
the nation. As we prepare to do so, let me prime the pump on a few
big ideas for your consideration:

- **Child care is education. And education is a public good.**
  If you take nothing else away from this chapter, let it be
  this: America's private early education market has failed—
  catastrophically and demonstrably—on multiple fronts.

  First, neither the public nor the industry has, to date,
  adequately conceptualized child care as what it is: one of
  humankind's most important drivers of human potential. And
  our failure to fully leverage human capital during the most
  formative years of development comes at untold cost to our
  society, economy, and global competitiveness.

  What's more, child care has failed to demonstrate its
  ability to deliver even the basic health and safety on which
  it is premised. Independent of any loftier goals, child care's
  business model is irreparably broken. It is a house of cards,
  premised on astronomical fees, questionable quality, and the
  exploitation of a low-wage workforce.

  The solution is plain: *The time has come for us to elevate early
  education's status to that of public good.* What that might look like,
  as I'll unpack in the next chapter, is open to further debate.
  But in the absence of transformative public funding, we will
  never resolve child care's current conundrum. The good news
  is that we're already paying for it—we're just doing it in all the
  wrong ways.
- **Compensation is key and should be the very first thing
  subsidized.** As we transition to a more publicly funded
  system of early care and education, it will be important to
  triage the system's most pressing need. That need is workforce
  compensation.

  At a median wage of $13.71 an hour, child care is at
  imminent risk of collapse, setting off an inevitable domino
  effect on our state and federal economies as parents are
  forced out of the workforce. At the bare minimum, it is
  incumbent upon policymakers (as a stopgap on the path
  toward more professional wages) to step in to keep wages
  competitive with those of other low-wage employers such
  as fast food restaurants and big box stores. We are already
  seeing classrooms sit vacant and longstanding programs

close their doors as programs struggle to attract qualified job applicants. Should this trend accelerate, expect more programs to shutter.

To those who insist it is not the place of government to intervene in the wages of private businesses, I point you to agriculture, banking, airlines, the automotive industry, and more. *Child care is too big to fail.* And eventually we're going to realize it.

CHAPTER 4

How *Not* to Solve the Child Care Crisis

Imperfect Solutions and Policy Pitfalls

Perhaps you've heard of Occam's razor—a logical principle attributed to medieval philosopher William of Occam—which dictates that the simplest explanation or solution is usually correct. There's little question (when it comes to public policy, at least) that the simplest solutions often garner the most enthusiastic support. But complex problems rarely have simple solutions. As the great American essayist H. L. Mencken (1920, p. 158) once noted, there is "a well-known solution to every human problem—neat, plausible, and wrong."

Such is the case with child care, an industry in which our collective misunderstanding of the problem routinely leads to "solutions" that actually exacerbate the field's challenges; in which *poison*—with all the best of intentions—is accidentally prescribed as a cure.

Having established child care as an industry in crisis, this book will dedicate its remaining chapters to the resolution of these challenges, beginning here with a set of cautionary tales in which we will unpack the dangers of common practices with the potential to sink the industry. What follows is a list of pitfalls to avoid—forms of public policy so egregious in their error that no serious discussion of the path forward can be undertaken without first taking them off the table. As we go, I'll share specific, actionable steps to address each pitfall, both within the chapter and in its closing Bipartisan Blueprint for Change.

PUBLIC POLICY PITFALLS

Pitfall 1: Overreliance on Public School Districts (or Why Mixed Delivery Matters)

Let me be crystal clear to avoid even the tiniest bit of confusion: As a former teacher and school district administrator, I am not here to criticize the nation's public schools, nor their early childhood programs (many, if not most of which, are simply terrific). From a public policy perspective, however, school districts' incursion into the early childhood marketplace—even when limited to prekindergarten for 3- and 4-year-olds—can quickly become an existential crisis for local child care providers, threatening the availability of infant-toddler care for millions of working families.

To understand why this is such an issue, we need to delve a little more deeply into the child care industry's precarious financial model. In the previous chapter we discussed the challenges of running a child care business, noting the industry's high overhead and staffing costs. Nowhere is this more problematic than in the provision of infant care, where the ratio of adults to children is so low—and associated costs so high—that child care businesses routinely struggle to break even in these classrooms. Think of infant care like one of those Black Friday doorbuster deals before the holidays: a costly product sold at a loss in hopes of getting you into the store to purchase something more profitable.

In infant classrooms, ratios are commonly in the 1:4 range, with one adult to every four babies, and most classrooms topping out at a maximum of 8 children. This makes good sense, of course. Given the unique needs of infants for one-on-one stimulation, feeding, and care, it's hard to imagine a single adult attempting to meet the needs of more than four babies. Frankly, the idea of meeting the needs of *more than one* is enough to make most new parents shudder.

Where child care businesses actually make their money (balancing out the deficits created by infant-toddler care) is with older preschoolers—3-, 4-, and 5-year-olds who can be served in larger numbers, often in classrooms of 20 or more—and with more budget-friendly staffing ratios, typically ranging from 1:8 to 1:10.

This brings us to the public policy challenge created by the expansion of public prekindergarten, which has grown increasingly ubiquitous across recent decades. Unlike K–12 education, early childhood has not traditionally been the wheelhouse of the nation's public schools, with a diverse ecosystem of private, community- and faith-based preschool providers historically filling this role.

Knowing what you now do, it's easy to understand why public school prekindergarten classrooms (sometimes referred to as "Universal Pre-K" or "transitional kindergarten")—independent of their quality and admirable intent—threaten to topple child care's already precarious business model. Left, in many communities, with increasingly fewer 4- and 5-year-old students, child care providers are slowly but surely losing access to the very students who enable their solvency.

It's a classic example of the *law of unintended consequences*, which dictates that the actions of people—and governments—"always have effects that are unanticipated or unintended" (Norton, n.d.), and a prime reason that policymakers need to proceed with caution when expanding public investment.

Circumspection, however, does not mean failure to act. As outlined in Chapter 2, high-quality prekindergarten programs provide one of public policy's strongest returns on investment. The real question here is not whether to invest, but *how these programs are best delivered.*

The solution is "mixed delivery"—which is the creation of public-private partnership models through which the same community-based providers who have historically served the nation's young children are eligible to receive public funding to expand service delivery *on behalf of the state*. Mixed-delivery models don't typically exclude public schools, but neither do they rely too heavily on them. The resulting parental choice model allows eligible families to select the public or private preschool provider that best meets their needs, without threatening the availability of services to younger children, currently provided almost exclusively in the private sector.

Most state prekindergarten systems now operate as mixed delivery models—*at least in theory*—though it's important to note that not all such systems are created equally. One determining factor is the role of school districts in governing the participation of their private-sector peers. Left to their own devices in state law to partner (*or not partner*) with private preschool providers, districts often choose the latter . . . or may establish token partnerships with a handful of preferred providers, rather than allowing private-sector preschools to flourish and thrive in this space.

A preferable structure may be like that of South Carolina, in which the participation of private-sector preschool providers is governed outside of the State Department of Education, with dollars earmarked separately in the state budget to underwrite the participation of both school districts and private providers, thus ensuring the robust participation of each. (In the interest of full disclosure, know that I played a hand in creating and administering South Carolina's mixed-delivery system, which I will nonetheless argue is the nation's best suited to ensure the strength and vitality of private sector providers.)

The primary lesson here, for policymakers and school district officials alike, is to be mindful of the inadvertent but potentially devastating effects caused by public schools entering into competition with an essential—but already desperately challenged—private market.

As a final aside here, it's important to recognize that different communities have very different needs and resources. One place where school districts may be an ideal service provider is in rural communities, which often lack sufficient population and demand to support a robust private preschool market. Even in such communities, districts are wise to proceed with caution, inviting community-based preschool providers (including home-based child care providers) into their planning processes in order to ensure they do no harm.

Pitfall 2: If You Build It, They Will Come (or the Perils of Creating Demand Without Supply)

"If you build it, they will come."

You might recognize the saying above as a popular misquote of a line from the baseball fantasy film *Field of Dreams*. In it, Kevin Costner plays an Iowa farmer who, urged on by a mysterious voice, builds a baseball diamond in a cornfield, attracting the ghosts of baseball legends of the past. The actual quote is "If you build it, *he* will come"—a reference to the character's deceased father—but that hasn't stopped the first variation from taking on a life of its own, often as an inspiration to entrepreneurs hoping to find an audience for a new product or service.

In the context of child care, the saying offers important guidance—and a major caution—to policymakers seeking to expand access. Which brings us back to the concepts of supply and demand. In the previous chapter we discussed how child care's broken fiscal model makes it different from many other businesses—and why strong demand for the service doesn't necessarily equate to a robust supply. In recent years, state policymakers have found this out the hard way.

Let's use the state of Michigan as a case study here. As the COVID-19 pandemic began to eat away at both labor participation and families' economic stability, the state decided to prioritize the use of federal pandemic relief dollars for a noble purpose: making child care more accessible and affordable to parents. By temporarily increasing eligibility for child care subsidy supports (raising the maximum family income from 150% of the federal poverty definition to 185%), the state envisioned making child care assistance available to significantly more families.

In the end, however, utilization fell well short of this goal.

"There were over 100,000 more families that became eligible for the subsidy as a result of increased funding for the program, but we really didn't see pick-up rates improve to a great extent," explained Karen Kling, strategic projects manager with University of Michigan's Poverty Solutions program (Powell, 2022).

The reason?

"They were pushing families toward spots that didn't exist."

The state was creating demand without supply. A similar situation played out in Oregon, where the state budgeted funding to expand its free Preschool Promise program to an additional 2,800 four-year-olds during the 2022–2023 school year. How many more children did they actually serve? About 500, according to data from the state's Early Learning Division (Wong, 2022). The culprit? A shortage of qualified teachers to staff these new classrooms.

In the abstract, you might think that the availability of millions of dollars in public funding would bring child care entrepreneurs crawling out of the woodwork. But that's not always true of a business in which profits range from slim to none. And it may be even less true in the case of prospective teachers who now have the ability to make not only more—but *substantially more*—in lower-stress, entry-level jobs elsewhere.

Indeed, existing classrooms are sitting vacant as you read these words, not because consumers don't desire (and, in many cases, *desperately need*) child care, but because there simply aren't adults willing to work for the pay these businesses are able to offer.

The case of First Baptist Church in El Dorado, Kansas, offers a sobering example. A fixture in the community for more than 6 decades, the church announced the closure of its beloved preschool program in August 2022 (KAKE, 2022). Was it because church leaders had lost their desire to continue the program? No. Was it because of lack of community demand for their services? No. In fact, the program maintained a waiting list of more than 100 families clamoring for one of *52 vacant slots* at the time of the program's closure. The problem was that the program literally couldn't field a teaching staff—receiving a total of *zero applications* for posted employment vacancies during the 3 months prior to its closure decision.

Just how bad is child care's access challenge becoming as a result of this disconnect between supply and demand? In rural Astoria, Oregon, Bumble Preschool and Arts Academy Director Amy Atkinson reports a surprising new phenomenon: parents adding frozen embryos to her program's waiting list in advance of their (open-ended) implantation (Rush, 2022).

It's that bad. But don't take it from me. Here are the words of a North Carolina child care director, with whom I spoke recently:

> It used to be that I'd advise parents to get on my program's waiting list the day they learn they are expecting . . . Now I tell them to call me if they have a hot date.

The lesson for policymakers is clear: The solution to the child care crisis involves more than creating increased demand. In a broken market it is insufficient—and frankly cruel—to promise parents greater access to a service that neither exists in sufficient supply, nor is likely to without public intervention. Real solutions will require the creation of both supply *and* demand.

Never forget the business advice imparted in Kevin Costner's cornfield: When it comes to child care, you have to *build it* before they can come.

Pitfall 3: Federal Malpractice (or How Market Rate Surveys Systematically Undermine the Stability of the Child Care Industry)

In the opening of this chapter, I described the topics to be covered as sometimes egregious errors with the potential to sink the child care industry. But there are a few that really take the cake—practices so widespread and detrimental that I can only describe them as forms of public policy malpractice. One such example is the use of market rate surveys.

Let me give you a little background.

Under the federal Child Care and Development Block Grant (CCDBG) Act, states are allocated funding via the Child Care and

Development Fund (CCDF) to provide child care subsidies for low-income working families. Most of these dollars are passed directly to child care providers on behalf of income-eligible families.

The CCDBG (2014) is, on paper at least, grounded in equal access, with the goal of promoting "parental choice to empower working parents to make their own decisions regarding the child care services that best suit their family's needs." The law spells out multiple components of equal access, ranging from states' efforts to address the needs of different geographic regions, to their efforts to link rates with program quality, to the affordability of parent co-payments (Bipartisan Policy Center, 2020b). But perhaps most important of all, the law requires states to justify the rates at which they reimburse providers using a "market rate survey or alternative methodology" (CCDBG, 2014).

A market rate survey is just what its name implies. States survey child care providers to determine the tuition rates paid by unsubsidized families and then use these data to help inform the rates at which they will reimburse providers for service to children receiving subsidized enrollment. On its face, this practice makes reasonably good sense. But the federal government *doesn't require states to pay these market rates . . .* or anything near them.

Instead, it recommends that they set their rates at no less than the 75th percentile of the market rate (meaning, in theory, that a subsidy should cover the cost of care at 75% of local child care businesses) and considers them out of compliance with the equal access requirement only when they dip *beneath the 50th percentile.* Not that any of this really matters, mind you, as 11 states have their rates set below—and in some cases *far below*—the 50th percentile at the time of this writing (see Figure 4.1), leaving low-income parents limited to the very cheapest (and often worst) providers in the market and/or leaving providers in the position of accepting far less than their going rates to serve low-income children (a practice that results in the refusal of many top providers to participate in state subsidy systems at all).

Let's take a step back, for a moment, and reflect upon what we already know about market rates. In Chapter 3 we established that even top market rates (at their hypothetical 99th percentile) are generally premised on a minimum wage workforce, laboring without health or retirement benefits. We also established that these same market rates often yield program owners a profit of 1% or less.

At current market rates, child care is on the brink of collapse, which is why the federal government's go-to methodology borders on unconscionable. Knowing that these rates are insufficient even at their upper

Figure 4.1. CCDF Lead Agency Reported Infant Payment Rates Expressed as a Market Rate Percentile

State	Infant (Center-Based)	Infant (Family Child Care)
Arizona	27th percentile	13th percentile
Colorado	25th percentile	25th percentile
Connecticut	45th percentile	44th percentile
Delaware	17th percentile	18th percentile
Georgia	25th percentile	25th percentile
Illinois	42nd percentile	72nd percentile
Indiana	26th percentile	40th percentile
Massachusetts	30th percentile	65th percentile
Minnesota	49th percentile	42nd percentile
Missouri	25th percentile	25th percentile
Ohio	25th percentile	25th percentile
Wyoming	40th percentile	55th percentile

Source: U.S. Department of Health and Human Services, Office of Child Care, 2023

limits, it is unacceptable not just to allow, but to tacitly encourage (through its 75th percentile recommendation) states to pay less. Here, it is no exaggeration to suggest that the federal government, through its own policy, is actively exacerbating the instability of the child care market. Something has to change.

Fortunately, there is hope on the horizon. While the CCDBG Act references market rate surveys explicitly—making them something that only Congress (and not the U.S. Department of Health and Human Services) has the authority to eliminate—this verbiage also allows states to set rates through use of "an alternative methodology, such as a cost estimation model, that has been developed by the State lead agency" (CCDBG, 2014).

While only a handful of states have had alternate methodologies approved as of this writing, cost estimation models are currently gaining traction. So, what are they and why might they be a superior approach?

Unlike market rate surveys, which looks only at the prices paid by parents for unsubsidized care, cost estimation models provide a far more complex—and accurate—portrait of the operating costs, pressures, and revenue drivers that influence the sustainability of child care businesses. Through the development of such models, states are able to examine how an array of factors might impact provider revenues and expenses, as well as how program characteristics (including group size, ratios, and staff qualifications) affect the real cost of delivering care.

Importantly, cost estimation models aren't necessarily tethered to the status quo. How might a rate premised on the provision of living wages for staff differ from a market rate dependent on poverty-level subsistence? A cost estimation model can tell you the answer. It may not always be the answer policymakers want to hear, but there's little question that this method provides a more accurate assessment of reality.

To be clear, neither market rate surveys nor cost estimation models ensure the adequacy of rates. Each is a tool to help guide action on the parts of the states, and each may provide valuable information. But one measures primarily what is (e.g., what parents can afford), whereas the other meaningfully informs what should be. Without cost estimation, policymakers are shooting in the dark.

What might such a transition mean for providers? In July 2023, following a cost estimation study, the New Mexico Early Childhood Education & Care Department discovered that their reimbursement rates for some enrolled children were off by *more than $200 per month* (O'Hara, 2023) when measured against the state's actual costs of care. With the benefit of the newly enabled public funding described in Chapter 2, the state was able to reconcile its rates with the true cost of quality, increasing rates across the board.

The time has come for policymakers across the nation to follow New Mexico's lead, to come to grips with the true costs of quality and act accordingly. Abandoning use of market rate surveys and eliminating reimbursement rates set substantially below those paid by unsubsidized parents are critical first steps.

Pitfall 4: Basing Reimbursement on Attendance

There's little question that low reimbursement rates destabilize our already fragile child care market. But they're not the only way that states undermine the solvency of child care businesses. Indeed, it is not uncommon for states to disburse these already low ball payments on the basis of each child's actual attendance.

Again, the practice seems reasonable enough. When making a purchase, we all want to pay for services actually rendered. But as with many things in the child care arena, there are important shades of gray to be considered. Do we want taxpayers footing the bill for a child who hasn't set foot in their classroom for months on end? Clearly not. But what about a child who misses three days due to the flu? Or whose family has to travel out of state unexpectedly due to the death of a loved one? Or whose car won't start? Believe it or not, these are all circumstances that can diminish the revenue of child care programs.

The more you understand, the less the practice makes sense. After all, these absences don't appreciably decrease provider costs. Classrooms must remain staffed. The lights remain on, and the rent is still due, even when individual children log absences. If there's a silver lining from COVID-19 for child care, it may be the way the pandemic helped to illuminate the folly of this practice, with virtually all states enacting emergency policies to transition away from attendance-based reimbursement, at least at the height of the public health crisis (The Hunt Institute, 2021b).

In the interim, a growing number of states have amended their policies to make enrollment-based reimbursement their new standard, permitting a reasonable number of absences before children are disenrolled and replaced on classroom rosters, but no longer penalizing child care businesses for absences that are wholly out of their control. If yours isn't one of them, it's time to act on this commonsense reform.

Pitfall 5: Adjustment of Adult: Child Ratios and Group Sizes (or Three Simple Truths? *What Three Simple Truths?*)

If there's one policy pitfall that cuts right to the very heart of the Daycare Myth, it is the temptation to increase adult:child ratios. The argument goes something like this: Child care businesses are struggling to keep their doors open and remain solvent. If we didn't regulate them so tightly and allowed them to serve more children per teacher (or classroom), we'd be doing them a great favor.

In all of public policy, you will never hear a bigger cop-out.

Of course, ratios and group sizes are topics that each state system must address. But to loosen established requirements as a primary solution to your state's child care's challenges is to undermine both the safety and development of its young children. It is an abdication of duty and a message to taxpayers that you'd prefer to saddle them with decades of costly consequences rather than lead in the here and now.

Meanwhile, it's not a fiscal solution either. A few more children may (or may not) help ward off closure in the short term, but this strategy will only keep child care limping along. It's not going to resolve the field's wage crisis, nor will it transform a teetering business into a thriving enterprise. At best, it is a metaphorical Band-Aid on a gaping head wound.

Ultimately, the ratio conversation brings us right back to the question of what these programs exist to provide. If your answer is basic health and safety, then go ahead . . . pack them full and pray for the best. But if you've learned anything across the past four chapters, I hope it is this: America's early childhood classrooms are not kennels. They are the learning laboratories in which many American children will either develop and strengthen the brain architecture, skills, and dispositions that will serve them well across decades . . . or not. It's really that simple.

Would allowing one additional baby per teacher (or three additional 2-year-olds) impact the safety of the children involved? If your answer is no, chances are good you've never been responsible for concurrently supervising half a dozen toddlers. But for the sake of argument, let's take the safety question off the table and focus solely on optimal development. This is an ideal time to offer a refresher on *The Three Simple Truths* introduced in Chapter 1.

The Three Simple Truths of Early Development

(1) Learning begins in utero and never stops.
(2) The period from prenatal to age 3 is a uniquely consequential window of human development during which the fundamental architecture of the brain is "wired."
(3) Optimal brain development is dependent on stable, nurturing relationships with highly engaged adults.

While all three are certainly applicable to this conversation, I'd like to focus here on the third of these truths, which is that optimal development is dependent on stable, nurturing relationships with highly engaged adults. Put plainly, babies need attention. *Lots and lots of attention.* And with each additional child in the care of an individual teacher comes a proportional decline in that adult's ability to provide it, suboptimizing the development not only of these additional children, but of each child in her care.

Knowing what we do about the long-term benefits of high-quality early childhood programs, the adjustment of ratios and group sizes (as an alternative to the provision of requisite public support) is a penny-wise, pound-foolish approach to policy—another payday loan scenario in which an immediate problem is remedied (though not really) at the highest long-term cost to children, families, and taxpayers. It's a cop-out, plain and simple.

Do child care businesses need additional revenue to stabilize their operation? Absolutely. But loosening ratios and group size is not the way. Even from a fiscal standpoint, it is—at best—tinkering around the edges in place of real reform. Don't fall into this trap.

Pitfall 6: Relying on Private Equity to Fill the Void

In the previous chapter, I shared my belief that most child care businesses are labors of love, small family businesses run by owners with a greater calling to service than motive for financial gain. I mean, given child care's broken financial model, this would almost have to be the case, right? But it isn't. At least not always.

Among the ranks of America's child care providers is also a growing threat: private equity. By private equity I mean large chains—some even publicly traded—whose motivations are, by definition, to turn child care centers into profit-making machines. If, knowing what you do about the industry's challenges, this idea strikes you as the last thing child care needs, you're not alone. That's because when one leg of child care's "three-legged stool" decides to pursue its interests differently, one or both of the other legs are inevitably going to be wobbling.

When it comes to the workforce, it's hard to imagine private equity firms making the situation a whole lot worse than it already is. After all, minimum wage *is* minimum wage. And in some cases, these chains actually pay comparatively well. Not *well*, mind you, but comparatively well. What's more, the quality of these programs doesn't always suffer in the ways you might expect. Indeed, some of these national chains even boast impressive accreditation figures.

But for parents, the growing market share of these for-profit providers can only play out in one way: higher costs. How much higher? At the time of this writing, one national chain garners $44,000 a year in Seattle. Another charges $40,000 in Manhattan (Goldstein, 2022). Oh, and this is the cost for *one child.*

If you're reading this and thinking, "I don't even *make* $44,000 a year," you're right to be alarmed. But then, you're really not the target audience. The point here is to cater to a small slice of the market capable of generating profits of 15% to 20% annually, as opposed to the 1% estimated by the Minneapolis Federal Reserve as more common in the field (Grunewald & Davies, 2011).

Where others see crisis, the chains see opportunity, opening a reported 537 new centers in 2022 and now serving a little over 8% of the
overall child care market (Goldstein, 2022). Indeed, as family-owned
businesses make the difficult decision to shut their doors, the chains are
often lying in wait, snatching up their programs for a song and imple-
menting steep tuition increases. But again, only in markets where this
approach makes sense. You won't find many of these businesses popping
up in rural areas or in low-income communities of color where their astronomical rates can't be sustained—which is ultimately the problem.

We already know that the free market can't easily generate the
access and affordability required by America's working parents. But
these chains don't aspire to any such calling. Instead, they exist to serve
a niche and uniquely well-heeled clientele. As such they aren't a solution to the nation's child care crisis, but rather an opportunistic force
capitalizing (both literally and figuratively) on the absence of a more
holistic solution.

Pitfall 7: Employer On-Site Child Care and Other Employer-Paid Benefits

As we move toward the completion of this chapter's list of policy pitfalls, I'd like to close out by addressing a couple of practices that argu-
ably do not rise to the same level of malpractice described above but
that can be problematic nonetheless. I'm speaking here of the role of
employers in providing child care. I'll break this section into two parts:
the provision of on-site care and the provision of employer-paid child
care benefits.

On both questions, you may find that I take a more pragmatic position than many advocates—welcoming the involvement of the business community, but also hoping to situate its appropriate role within
the context of this book's broader conversation.

So, let's jump right in.

Employer on-site child care. Should employers create on-site child
care programs for their employees? The answer is complex, ultimately defying a simple yes or no answer. Across decades in early childhood policy, I've gained an appreciation for the power of coalitions.
Accordingly, my general approach is to welcome anyone willing to
come to the table in good faith . . . and that very much includes the
business community (which, as you learned in Chapter 2, is feeling the
impact of the child care crisis on its own bottom line in much the same
way parents are).

Struggling not only to attract and retain employees, but also to maintain productivity and profitability, a growing number of employers are creating on-site child care programs. These programs offer parents a ton of convenience and in many instances the opportunity to visit (and even breastfeed) their children periodically throughout the day. You won't find me arguing against the benefits here.

Further, on-site child care can be both a boon and a necessity for certain types of employers. With most community-based child care programs limited to weekday business hours, Monday through Friday, hospitals and industrial employers who rely heavily on shift work and around-the-clock production, 7 days a week, may actually find it difficult to attract employees without accommodating on-site care. So, what's not to like?

Nothing inherently. But as with the discussion of the role of school districts that opened this chapter, on-site programs come with important cautions around *fit*. First, there is the question of organizational fitness. As we've worked to establish throughout this book, early childhood programs are about more than convenience and custodial care. They are critical early learning environments, requiring well-qualified and appropriately compensated staff. Not only are they difficult to run—often requiring expertise and skill sets that are not the specialties of the businesses seeking to create these facilities on-site—but highly regulated and notoriously unprofitable . . . especially when designed around both the developmental needs of young children and the provision of living wages to staff. These are not limitations you'd want to discover only after opening an on-site facility, so it's important that employers enter into such conversations with their eyes wide open. Child care is not something businesses can provide casually.

Then there's the question of fit within the community. The key consideration: What is the impact of opening an employer-operated center on the rest of the local child care ecosystem? Like school districts before them, large community employers entering the marketplace have the potential to destabilize existing providers, draining enrollment and revenue off struggling programs.

In the end, the relative wisdom of offering on-site care is a decision to be considered on a case-by-case basis, with careful attention to the potential cost, organizational fit, and impact of each proposed program on the larger community. For a whole host of reasons, employers may find that they are better served—both financially and organizationally—by offering their employees stipends for use within existing community programs, rather than creating new child care programs of their own.

Which brings us to the employee benefits question, also somewhat controversial in the policy space.

Employer-paid child care benefits. Especially in the current climate, no one—and I mean *no one*—wants to argue against employers voluntarily stepping in to provide benefits that make child care more affordable and accessible for their employees. Indeed, such employers are to be celebrated and held up as models (particularly in cases where they successfully *sustain* these programs, which is not always a given).

But at the macro level, the practice raises an important question about the future of early childhood in this country: *Is early childhood education a public good* (as I have argued previously and will continue throughout this book's closing chapter) *worthy of public funding for all children?* Or is it destined to become more and more like health care, with access and quality largely tied to the whims and budgets of individual employers? It's a hard question to answer because it pits an idealized future state against (undoubtedly well-intentioned) relief in the here and now.

But this book wasn't written to celebrate Band-Aids. Indeed, it is my hope that it sparks conversation about the wholesale transformation of America's early childhood landscape, which is why an honest discussion here is essential.

No matter how well-intended and beneficial they may be to the families receiving them, at the systems level, employer-funded child care benefits threaten to send us down the wrong path. Is it a better path than the one we're on now? For some families—those employed by the large corporate employers most likely to offer them—the answer is probably yes. But for those struggling most to access and afford early childhood education, those in low-wage positions already lacking the employer-compensated health and retirement benefits that only the privileged accept as commonplace, the answer is an unqualified no. And that's unlikely to ever change, unless and until we act as a nation.

What does this mean in the short term? Here there may be a special two-pronged opportunity for those business owners thoughtful enough to provide child care benefits now because it's the right thing to do for their employees: (1) plow ahead, continuing and expanding the provision of short-term supports, and (2) join others in speaking out about the need for such benefits to be made available *to all families.*

Inevitably the question will arise as to whether businesses are willing to play a role in helping to support a universal benefit, and no one's voice will be more credible than business owners who are already putting their money where their mouth is.

We'll talk more about the future of child care in the next chapter.

THE BIPARTISAN BLUEPRINT FOR CHANGE

Parents and Professionals

Because this chapter is heavy on policy (and therefore *policymakers*), I'm going to address parents and professionals with some similar words of guidance here. What you've just read is not a hypothetical list of public policy pitfalls—ideas that *might* become problematic if they were ever to be enacted. Sadly, the practices I've laid out over the preceding pages are very much the norm. Indeed, it's likely not a question of *whether* your state relies on some of them, but just *how many?*

Perhaps the most important thing to keep in mind here is how sensible some of these "solutions" appear at first glance. Especially among policymakers unfamiliar with the challenges currently facing the child care industry, these approaches are often enacted as good-faith efforts to support families and providers. It's not until you dig deeper to understand their unintended consequences that their danger becomes evident, which is where *you* come in.

It is critical that policymakers understand the impact of their work, especially when public policy actually serves to undermine the very goals it exists to serve. Are the practices described above negatively impacting your business (or your child's preschool)? If so, it's time to speak up. Schedule time for a conversation with your state-elected leaders. If you don't know who they are, most states have simple online search tools that will help you find your elected House and Senate members. If you don't reach them directly, leave a message asking to schedule a time to speak (as opposed to just a message outlining your concerns). Solicit a dialogue and build relationships.

And because child care policy is typically under the purview of a gubernatorial cabinet agency, don't forget to include direct outreach to your governor's office. When you call, they're highly unlikely to put you through to the governor personally, but do push past the receptionist. Ask who within the administration is the main point of contact for child care issues and ask for a few minutes with them, even if this needs to be scheduled for a later time.

When you do get the chance to connect, tell your story, being as specific as possible about how state policies are impacting the quality of care you provide or receive, destabilizing the availability of early care and education, and/or influencing your bottom line (either as a business or as a family). Your conversation partner may not have detailed knowledge of the subject, so avoid jargon and acronyms and explain yourself thoroughly. As you do, assume that everyone you speak with is ready to help address the issue in good faith. Not all of them will, of course, but there's no better way to make sure your message *isn't* heard than taking on an aggressive, accusatory, or excessively partisan tone.

For extra guidance on this topic, see Appendix B: Reaching Out to Your Elected Leaders: A How-To for Parents and Professionals.

Put simply, ask for help. And equip your policymakers with the information they need to intervene on your behalf. You may be surprised by the outcome. For elected officials, constituent service is often the difference between a single term in office and the chance to continue serving. And even if your conversation doesn't lead to immediate action, you will have educated them in ways likely to ripple across their future actions.

Policymakers

If you're a policymaker still reading this deep in the book, I'm going to assume that you're ready to be an agent of change in your state. So let's talk about how.

In the next chapter I'll wrap things up with a discussion of proactive changes with the power to transform the nation's early childhood landscape. But I also don't want you to lose sight of opportunities to correct errors of the past—errors that may still be dragging your system down and making life difficult for both the families and early childhood service providers you have been elected to serve.

Put simply, your state's early childhood system needs a checkup. And you're just the person to conduct it, using the seven pitfalls outlined in this chapter as a guide. To that end, here is a list of issues and guiding questions for you to consider.

- *Mixed delivery and the role of school districts.* Recognizing the danger posed by school districts' incursion into the early childhood marketplace, there's no better time than the present to ensure that public investments aren't inadvertently undermining the cost and availability of infant/toddler programs. Here's what you'll want to discern:

» First, if your state invests in public prekindergarten, who is eligible to provide services? If the answer is limited to school districts, this should be a giant red flag.

» If both school districts and private/community-based providers have an opportunity to serve, you have the makings of a true mixed-delivery system. But not all such systems are created equal. The key question here is: *Who gets to decide whether and how private providers participate?* If the answer is school districts, you'll want to dig deeply to ensure the private sector's meaningful participation. *How many such partnerships exist? And what percentage of enrolled children are served in private settings?* (You might be surprised to learn how little mixed delivery actually happens in your state's so-called mixed-delivery system.)

» Then ask yourself: *Does it have to be this way? How might state law be changed to better ensure the robust participation of private sector providers? Might separate line items in the state budget help to protect child care providers and prevent school districts from gobbling up more than their fair share of the early childhood marketplace?*

» Another question to explore relates to funding equity. It's not uncommon for states to fund prekindergarten programs at levels far lower than their true cost. For school districts, which are often able to tap into other sources of public funding to cover the difference—and for whom capital costs and utilities are already covered— this can be a manageable nuisance. But for private-sector providers without these benefits, insufficient state funding can be a deal-breaker. *Does your state provide differential rates for public and private providers designed to help bolster private-sector participation and protect infant/ toddler care? Might you exempt participating providers from property taxes (or other fiscal burdens) to help level the playing field?*

» Finally, recognize that many districts act independently of the state in this regard, using locally generated revenue or discretionary dollars to expand early childhood programs on their own volition. *What role might you, as an elected official, play in shaping and monitoring these plans to prevent such well-intentioned efforts from crashing the local child care market?*

- **Avoiding the temptation to create demand without supply.** In the course of your duties, it's not unlikely that you'll be faced with proposals to address child care's growing access crisis with a simple solution: budgeting for more children to participate. Here it's important that you remain mindful that, when it comes to child care, *demand-side solutions routinely fail to deliver increased supply.*
  - » What you need instead are strategies to increase both supply and demand concurrently. *One such way is to couple expanded subsidy funding, for example, with funds designed to meaningfully increase teacher salaries.* Never expect that providers will be able to accommodate more children in the absence of more teachers. In the long term, these teachers need professional wages. In the short term, don't expect miracles of child care businesses that can't even compete for employees with Walmart and McDonald's.
- **Killing off your state's market rate survey.** One of the lowest-hanging fruits in this whole conversation is the elimination of market rate surveys as your state's method of setting child care subsidy rates. How do you find out if this remains your state's preferred method? It's easy: Reach out to your state's CCDF administrator (generally located within the cabinet agency charged with overseeing child care) and ask. Here's what you'll want to know:
  - » *Through what method does the state set its child care subsidy rates?* If through a market rate survey, *at what percentile are these rates currently set and when was the survey in question completed?* (You might be surprised to find that these rates are sometimes pegged to surveys that are already outdated by years.) The closer these rates are to the 99th percentile on a current survey, the more reasonable they will be—though keep in mind that even at the top of the market, these rates are routinely insufficient to provide living wages to staff.
  - » *Has the state considered pursuing an alternative methodology, such as a cost of care study?* If so, great. Ask what you can do to help support its implementation and approval. If

not, ask what supports the agency might need to move in this direction. (These studies are not typically very costly in the grand scheme of state budgets but may require some dedicated funding to get off the ground.)

  » If your state has already completed a cost of care study, *how do the state's current subsidy reimbursement rates compare to those identified as required by the study? How might you support the agency in building the political will to adjust them accordingly?*

  » While you're at it, be sure to inquire about *whether the state's subsidy reimbursement policies are based on attendance or enrollment.* If the former, find out what the agency needs from you to ensure it becomes the latter. *Is it growing political will? The provision of additional funding?* This is another low-hanging fruit.

- *Increasing adult:child ratios and group sizes.* This one is simple. *Not on your watch.* Don't propose increased ratios, and fight tooth and nail against any proposal that undermines the safety and optimal development of young children. Should you find that your state is more permissive here than other states, explore how to roll these ratios back to an acceptable norm.

  » While we're at it, know that there are often associated proposals to decrease the minimum age (and credentials) of those permitted to supervise children unattended, sometimes to 16 or younger. This is the Daycare Myth in action. Children watching children is not the solution. Don't fall for it.

CHAPTER 5

A Wholesale Transformation of America's Early Childhood Landscape

In the opening pages of this book, I shared the story of the U.S. Department of Agriculture's 1992 Food Pyramid, which provided guidance so far off-base that many experts believe it *actually contributed* to the obesity epidemic it sought to help curb by increasing Americans' intake of processed and refined carbohydrates—all the while fueling an ill-conceived $35 billion no-fat snack food industry (Pyanov, 2023). Anyone remember SnackWell's fat-free cookies? It turns out they weren't the key to healthy weight management after all.

More than 3 decades later, the Food Pyramid is not only a shining example of public policy gone awry, but also a cautionary tale regarding how such errors can happen at scale. Just *how did* the federal government end up promulgating guidance so egregiously inaccurate? Experts have identified at least two major flaws in the pyramid's development.

The first was an urge to make the complex simple. Even then, nutritionists were well aware of the distinctions between saturated and unsaturated fats, for example—just as they were aware of the meaningful differences between unrefined, naturally occurring carbohydrates (like the dietary fiber found in almonds) and highly processed sugars (like the high-fructose corn syrup added to soda). But these complexities don't lend themselves well to simple graphics and pithy messaging. In the end, simplicity won the day, obscuring any of a number of important nuances on the way to a message that mostly boiled down to *fat is bad and carbs are good* (Stampfer & Willett, 2006).

The other challenge was an inherent conflict of interest. Which is to say that the process was tracked, negotiated, and informed by lobbyists representing the very industries the U.S. Department of Agriculture exists not only to regulate, but *to subsidize and promote*: agriculture, livestock, and dairy (Nestle, 1993).

The parallels to our nation's disastrous early childhood policy are clear, and—as I've unpacked over the course of the preceding chapters—these same two errors contribute mightily to our nation's flawed approach to the early years.

There is little question that the Daycare Myth is rooted in oversimplification, leading policymakers and the public to conceive of early childhood, primarily, as a period of custodial caretaking. Willfully disregarding decades of brain science, *we continue to see what we have always seen*: child care as an industrialized form of babysitting and a mechanism through which to promote adult employment. As if stuck in the 1940s, the motivations underlying our early childhood investments have little to do with the optimal development of children and everything to do with their parents. It's not that parental employment is an unreasonable goal, mind you. It's that it's a conflict of interest—a different proposition altogether.

THE CURRENT EARLY CHILDHOOD POLICY PYRAMID

The result of the Daycare Myth is a disastrous pyramid of our own, depicted in Figure 5.1: an early childhood system grounded in a fundamental misunderstanding of the early years. Ours is a bizarro world in which:

- The most important window in all of human development is written off as inconsequential.
- Child care is inaccessible, unaffordable, and unprofitable.
- Low-wage women (many of them women of color) subsidize the workforce participation of millions.
- Public policy routinely serves to undermine, rather than promote, the stability of families and providers.
- Taxpayers are doomed to support the burdensome, long-term results of inaction, rather than the lower costs of proactive investment.

The solution is not an endless series of policy tweaks designed to make things just a little better around the edges. What we need is an

Figure 5.1. The Current Early Childhood Policy Pyramid

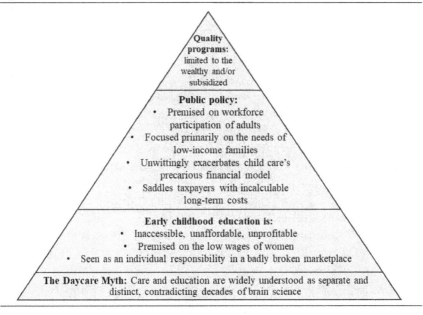

Quality programs: limited to the wealthy and/or subsidized

Public policy:
- Premised on workforce participation of adults
- Focused primarily on the needs of low-income families
- Unwittingly exacerbates child care's precarious financial model
- Saddles taxpayers with incalculable long-term costs

Early childhood education is:
- Inaccessible, unaffordable, unprofitable
- Premised on the low wages of women
- Seen as an individual responsibility in a badly broken marketplace

The Daycare Myth: Care and education are widely understood as separate and distinct, contradicting decades of brain science

inversion of this pyramid: a wholesale transformation of America's early childhood landscape. And the longer we wait to act, the more human potential we sacrifice and the more taxpayer dollars we waste.

So how do we get there?

The first step is a change in mindset, a paradigm shift away from the thinking of the past and a widespread recognition of early development as *the* critical determinant of children's academic and lifelong success. This is the conversation this book hopes to jumpstart, beginning with two simple changes—neither of which will cost a dime:

- The elimination of the terms *daycare* and *child care* from our collective vocabularies
- Recognition that environments in which children learn are *schools* and the adults who facilitate their learning are *teachers*

Will these semantic changes transform public policy overnight? Probably not. But what they will do is shine a spotlight on how shamelessly misguided—and poorly aligned with the interests of children—our policies actually are. And that's what we need to get the ball rolling.

The other thing systemic reform will require is public investment—significant, transformative public investment.

I can already hear some of you grumbling about big government spending. But let me assure you that what I'm proposing is very much the opposite. In fact, it is about *shrinking* the size of government and *diminishing* tax burden through—not an expansion—but a strategic *repositioning* of the social safety net.

You may be familiar with the term "nanny state," which has long been used in political circles as a derisive description of a government that devalues personal responsibility and is overly reliant on social programs (the implication being that in such systems, able-bodied adults must be supported as if they were children).

Ironically enough, few such supports exist for actual children—leaving the American public to shoulder steep costs across decades that could (and should) have been addressed during the earliest years of life. The time has come for us to acknowledge this approach as a self-fulfilling prophecy: *We live in a metaphorical nanny state due, in large part, to the absence of a literal nanny state.*

Suppose, instead, we made a national priority of shifting our sunk costs. Imagine if we dedicated ourselves to lowering the incalculable (and multigenerational) taxpayer burdens created by grade-level retention and remediation, special education, social service dependency, negative health outcomes, and interactions with the criminal justice system (all well-documented to be diminished by high-quality early childhood programs) by making smarter decisions about where we direct our dollars in the first place.

It wouldn't be an overnight fix. And, yes, it would likely cost more in the short term. But it begs a national conversation: Just how endlessly are we willing to pay for the results of our errors before we *acknowledge and correct the errors themselves?*

By committing ourselves to a generational repositioning of the social safety net—providing more ample supports to our youngest while diminishing the need for (and, thus, utilization of) taxpayer-funded services across the entirety of their life spans—it's not unreasonable to envision such a shift not only as revenue neutral, but as a significant long-term savings—enabling diminished tax burdens and a phased shrinkage in the overall size of government.

That should be something on which we can all agree—*Republican or Democrat.*

Figure 5.2. The New Early Childhood Policy Pyramid

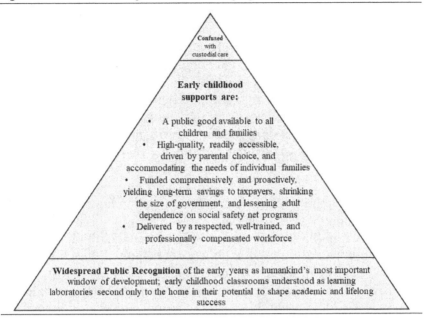

THE NEW EARLY CHILDHOOD POLICY PYRAMID

This brings us to a vision for the future: a new and improved early childhood policy pyramid (depicted in Figure 5.2) intended to right our historical wrongs and address the field's long-standing crises.

Grounded in widespread understanding of the early years as life-changing, our updated pyramid recognizes early childhood supports as a public good—as readily available to families as K–12 education, funded proactively and comprehensively, and delivered by a well-trained and professionally compensated workforce.

How do we get there, and what does the associated policy look like? The remainder of this chapter will be focused on answering this question and uplifting current state and federal models that hold promise as we envision a brighter future. Let me be clear that what follows is not a recipe, but rather a conversation starter. Indeed, my hope is that as state and federal policymakers advance this cause, their ideas—and yours—will far outstrip any of my own.

A Focus on the Child and the Promotion of Meaningful Family Choice

I want to make something clear: I am not here to advocate for a birth-to-5 equivalent to (or expansion of) the nation's public schools.

As I hope has become evident, my underlying concern is not about systems and structures; it is about *children and families*. So when I say that the nation needs transformative, public investment, I do not mean a government-run system in which children must enroll at 6 weeks. Indeed, I'm not necessarily an advocate for enrollment in *any program at all*.

Instead, let's start here: The years of early childhood are uniquely consequential, requiring safe and loving care, attentive interaction, and abundant opportunities to learn, play, and grow. Our goal should be ensuring that *these needs are met for every American child*.

How and where are these experiences best provided for your child? As far as I'm concerned, it's not my place to say. Nor is it that of government, which is why I am a believer in robust parental choice in this space—and why an ideal system would provide resources designed to support the needs of *both* working parents and those who may prefer to provide for this care, nurture, and learning directly, in the comfort of their own homes.

Meeting the Needs of Stay-at-Home Parents

In truth, as badly as we are failing the needs of working parents, we may be failing those of stay-at-home parents even worse—offering taxpayer-funded supports for parents willing to place their children in center-based programs, but precious little for those electing to stay at home with their children. What's worse, policymakers routinely speak out of both sides of their mouths when it comes to stay-at-home parents.

On one hand, I've encountered dozens and dozens of policymakers over the course of my career who insist that "a parent" (read: mothers) should stay at home with their young children. Often romanticizing their own upbringing in the *Leave It to Beaver* world of late-1950s maternal homemakers, they insist that out-of-home care is vastly inferior and that, if anything, public policy should be designed to support stay-at-home parents. (Not that they actually design it as such, mind you . . .)

On the other hand, it is often these same policymakers (seemingly without irony) who enact strict work requirements linked to any form of public benefit. The double standard is clear: Stay-at-home parenting is the preferred approach for upper-middle-class (typically white) mothers. All others, get a job.

It's time we said it straight: You can't have it both ways. It's another example of how America's "welfare-to-work" reforms ignore the well-being of children in their relentless pursuit of parental employment. It's time we learn to walk and chew gum at the same time, developing policies that promote not only employment and self-sufficiency, but the optimal development of children as well.

How might we better support *all families* in making the best choices for their children? We would begin with a robust system of paid parental leave, ensuring that one or both parents have the option of spending the most critical weeks and months of attachment, bonding, and brain development in the company of their babies.

From there, we might look at innovative approaches to tax policy. For example, might we provide parents the option of front-loading the lifetime value of the federal child tax credit during the years from 0 to 5 (as opposed to drawing upon it incrementally from 0 to 17), providing a more significant benefit to the parents of young children and enabling more of them to stay home during the early years (Stevens & Weidinger, 2021)?

And what about child care subsidies? Suppose we were to follow the lead of Minnesota, where parents are offered (for a total of 12 months) the option of drawing 68% of the reimbursement that might otherwise have gone to a center-based provider for the enrollment of their child (Minnesota Statutes, 2023). Might it help alleviate the nation's infant-care shortage? Could it make the difference between requiring infant care and being able to provide it yourself?

There's little question that we could do more as a nation to promote stay-at-home parenting for those who wish to choose this path. The reality, however, is that stay-at-home parenting is an economic luxury far beyond the reach of many American families. As a believer in parental choice, I'm not here to advocate for either approach as superior, but would note that we have a long way to go toward making stay-at-home parenting a viable option.

Meeting the Needs of Working Parents

With the caveat that public policy here should take a two-pronged approach (supporting both in-home *and* out-of-home supports), we are also in need of a vastly different system of service provision outside the home. With roughly two-thirds of American children currently re-siding in homes in which all available parents are participants in the workforce (Kids Count Data Center, 2021b), the need for a robust system of early childhood education beginning in infancy is a clear imperative.

Parental choice is critical here as well, which is another reason I'm skeptical of a public school system–type approach to birth to 5. This isn't to suggest that school systems don't have a role to play. But that role is as *one of many* service providers (alongside private, community- and faith-based preschools) in *a robust mixed-delivery system.* Which brings us to the opportunity to discuss another critical service provider.

Throughout this book, I've taken pains to spotlight the many ways that federal public policy is focused on the needs of adults and mis-aligned with those of children. But if you were paying careful atten-tion in the opening chapter, you may recall that I made reference to one notable exception to this rule. That exception is Head Start.

Created under the leadership of President Lyndon Johnson as an 8-week summer program in 1965, Head Start has grown and evolved over the intervening decades into an umbrella term covering a collec-tion of year-round, federally funded early childhood programs de-signed to address the needs of children in poverty, including Early Head Start (which serves children from prenatal to 3), the Head Start pre-school program (serving children ages 3–5), Migrant and Seasonal Head Start (targeting the children of migrant and seasonal agricultural workers), Tribal Head Start (serving the children of American Indians/ Alaska Natives), and more.

Though the program is frequently confused with state-funded pre-kindergarten, it's actually much more than a classroom-based inter-vention. Indeed, Head Start programs are designed to meet the holistic needs of participating children and their families, supplementing a high-quality classroom experience with comprehensive, wraparound services and supports, including nutritional and mental health services, parent education, connections to community resources, and more.

What's particularly notable about Head Start is the extent to which the program tackles, head-on, virtually all of the systemic challenges outlined in this book. The program has rigorous educational and safe-ty standards that far exceed those of most child care licensing systems, highly qualified teachers (who may soon achieve pay parity with those employed by public schools), and an evidence-based curriculum.

How do they manage to pull it off? The answer, which can only inform our path forward, is with *sufficient public funding.* Local Head

Start grantees are directly funded by the federal government at levels reflecting the true costs of the services they provide. Unlike the private child care market, in which parents, providers, and the workforce are all disadvantaged by a badly broken financial model, Head Start programs offer a glimpse of what high-quality early childhood programs might look like as a public good, rather than an individual luxury.

Notably, the initiative's recent Early Head Start–Child Care Partnerships model (in which Head Start services are provided within private child care businesses, rather than dedicated Head Start centers) has provided the nation with a much-needed template for how mixed delivery can work in the years prior to prekindergarten through the creation of public-private partnerships.

As in the case of public schools, it is not my intent to advocate for universal Head Start—or any single service provision model. But as a structure and a proof point, Head Start has much to offer. Interestingly enough, so too does the nation's military child care system, which is generally considered a model of quality. Both serve as instructive templates in which federal funds have been successfully deployed to create high-quality systems for some—*but not all*—American children. It's time we provide these and other high-quality options for all children.

Looking to Congress

Transforming America's early childhood landscape—equitably and at scale—is ultimately a job not for state legislatures, but for Congress. And despite Congress's well-deserved reputation as the nation's most polarized (and, thus, gridlocked) elected body, there remain glimmers of hope for a bipartisan solution.

Take the Biden administration's failed post-COVID Build Back Better (BBB) initiative, for example. As proposed by the administration and Democratic lawmakers in late 2021, BBB would have pumped transformative investments (totaling approximately $400 billion over 10 years) into the expansion of both child care access and universal prekindergarten for 3- and 4-year-olds. Among other provisions, the plan would have dramatically increased eligibility for federal child care subsidies (raising eligibility from the current income cutoff of 85% of state median income to 250% of the same), capped parent co-payments at no more than 7% of a family's annual household income (exempting the nation's lowest-income families from any co-payment at all), and providing significant infrastructure supports designed to increase child care supply (The Hunt Institute, 2021a).

While BBB was summarily dismissed along partisan lines in the U.S. Senate, a set of 15 Republican Senators led by South Carolina Senator (and 2024 Republican presidential candidate) Tim Scott introduced legislation proposing to reauthorize the Child Care and Development Block Grant in March 2022. Among the bill's provisions: (a) expansion of child care subsidy eligibility (from 85% to 150% of state median income), (b) capping co-payments at no more than 7% of a family's annual household income (while exempting lowest-income earners), and (c) providing significant infrastructure supports designed to increase child care supply (The Hunt Institute, 2022).

If those broad strokes sound surprisingly similar, then you're reading them correctly. To be clear, the bills were hardly identical in terms of scale, scope, and likely cost. BBB included universal prekindergarten and proposed guaranteed funding—whereas the Scott plan was focused exclusively on child care, had a narrower eligibility definition, and never advanced to the point of a specific funding proposal. But the makings of a significant bipartisan compromise are clearly evident.

It's important to note that President Biden's sweeping BBB plan included far more than just the early childhood provisions noted here—and ultimately failed as a result of its substantial total price tag, which some independent budget analyses pegged in excess of $2 trillion over 10 years (Funke, 2021). But were its early childhood investments themselves too costly?

The available evidence suggests that *they may not have been robust enough to even offset real-time losses to the American economy*. As proposed by the administration, BBB's child care and prekindergarten spending would have entailed a roughly $40 billion annualized investment over 10 years. Compare this to the $122 billion in annual losses to parents, employers, and state economies estimated by Ready Nation (Bishop, 2023) due to insufficient infant-toddler care, and you'll see the folly of it all. The bottom line: We're already paying the cost of transforming America's early childhood landscape . . . three times over.

It's time for Congress to act. And to act in ways commensurate with the scale of the problem.

PROMISING PRACTICES IN THE STATES

While nationwide reform ultimately sits on the shoulders of Congress, there's little question that the federal government's persistent inaction is felt most acutely by the states. No longer willing to stand on the sidelines as the child care crisis threatens the stability of families, businesses, and local economies, a growing number of states and territories are stepping up to the challenge—enacting innovative solutions that may serve as models for the nation. Below are a few recent examples that—*while stopping well short of defining early childhood as a public good*—offer signs of hope for a brighter tomorrow.

Solving the Compensation Crisis

Addressing the field's growing compensation crisis is job number one for policymakers. It's also the subject of an ideological divide, with many elected leaders expressing concern over the role of government in supporting the wages of private-sector employers.

But we've seen the damage caused by this approach, and I would again note here that the federal government *routinely* subsidizes the operation of industries deemed "too big to fail" (agriculture, airlines, automotive production, banks, and energy, just to name a few). It's not that the practice is actually so uncommon. *It's that early childhood education has yet to rise to this level of perceived importance among policymakers and the public.* But that's beginning to change.

Take Washington, DC, for example. Recognizing the District's growing challenge to attract and retain an early childhood workforce, the DC Council created the Early Childhood Educator Pay Equity Fund in August 2021 with the explicit purpose of enhancing compensation. Funded through a marginal tax increase on DC's highest-income earners (Weil & Brice-Saddler, 2021) and administered by the District's Office of the State Superintendent of Education, the fund is currently subsidizing child care salaries by an additional $14,000 annually for lead teachers and $10,000 annually for classroom assistants. In 2022, the District used proceeds from the Pay Equity Fund to take its efforts one step further, providing "access to free, quality, publicly financed health insurance coverage" for all of DC's child care staff and their families (Anbar-Shaheen, 2022).

It's worth noting that DC has also enacted some of the nation's most ambitious lead teacher requirements. After a contentious phase-in, the District now requires lead teachers to (a) possess an associate's degree (or higher) in early childhood education; (b) have completed 60 credit hours in an unrelated field, alongside at least 12 hours in early childhood education; or (c) demonstrate enrollment in a degree program and earn an associate's degree or higher within 4 years of their hiring.

What's notable about these efforts is the way they work hand in hand. DC has not only set a high bar for teachers but is also demonstrating its willingness to put its money where its mouth is to attract and retain them.

The District isn't alone in exploring solutions to the compensation crisis. Alabama, for example, recently piloted use of one-time federal COVID relief dollars to provide $3,000 quarterly bonuses ($12,000 annually) to the state's early childhood professionals (LeBerte, 2023), while New Mexico is using funds enabled under its November 2022 Constitutional Amendment to create pay parity between public- and private-sector teachers in the state's mixed-delivery prekindergarten program (New Mexico Early Childhood Education and Care Department, 2023) and raise lead teacher pay in child care settings to $20 an hour (Office of New Mexico Governor Michelle Lujan Grisham, 2022)—some $8 more than the state's minimum hourly wage.

Colorado and Louisiana, meanwhile, have taken novel approaches of their own—enacting refundable tax credits that bolster the income of directors and teachers. In Colorado, early childhood professionals can qualify for up to $1,500 annually, while in Louisiana this credit can reach $3,787 per year, dependent on teacher qualifications and years of experience (National Women's Law Center, 2023).

Solving the Affordability Crisis

Compensation isn't the only place New Mexico is leading the way. With healthy oil and gas revenues fueling the state's Land Grant Permanent Fund and anticipated support for the state's pending (and ultimately successful) Constitutional Amendment, the state used one-time pandemic relief funds boldly—with the expectation that they could be sustained. In April 2022, Governor Lujan Grisham joined with leadership of the state's Early Childhood Education and Care Department to announce that it would be waiving parent co-payments and raising the state's subsidy eligibility threshold to 400% of the federal poverty definition (approximately $111,000 per year for a family of four)—making the state the first to make child care free for nearly all families (Covert, 2022).

In 2023, Vermont took an equally ambitious swing at solving the child care crisis, passing legislation poised to generate upward of $120 million a year for the cause (Duffort, 2023). The new law enacts a small payroll tax primarily supported by employers (who will shoulder three-quarters of this cost), allowing the state to raise its eligibility definition for the receipt of subsidized care to 575% of the federal poverty definition

($172,500 by my math—$30.000 x 575%. annually for a family of four). While parents at the upper end of this spectrum are still subject to reasonable co-payments, there's little question that Vermont is taking big leaps forward. The common denominator in both New Mexico and Vermont, *transformative public funding,* cannot be overlooked.

Another trend beginning to impact child care affordability is the emergence of cost-sharing models. The brainchild of Michigan Representative Greg VanWoerkom, the state's Tri-Share model casts child care as a three-way partnership among parents, their employers, and the state—each of whom covers one-third of the overall cost. For many policymakers, the model holds significant appeal as it requires both families and the business community to have skin in the game, while enabling state support to three times as many children as might otherwise be served. At the time of this writing, variations on the Tri-Share model are currently being implemented/piloted (under a variety of state-specific names) in Kentucky, North Dakota, New York, and North Carolina, with more states currently exploring its feasibility.

Solving the Access Crisis

Though the two go hand in hand—or should at least—it's important to heed Chapter 4's reminder that affordability and access aren't one and the same. As you've learned, simply funding more subsidized child care slots doesn't necessarily translate to the availability of more of these slots in practice—which is why states such as New Mexico, Vermont, and North Dakota have all paired substantial expansion with improved subsidy reimbursement rates designed to help support increased supply. The Vermont legislation described above, for example, enacted an immediate 35% increase in child-care subsidy rates, *which may itself impact child care compensation* through the provision of more operating capital to providers.

States are also exploring innovative new ways to expand and stabilize child care's supply chain. In Connecticut, for example, a family child care incubator concept is currently being piloted (Putterman, 2024). The model co-locates family child care startups in a centralized facility akin to a shopping mall. Here each business operates as an independent storefront but shares in the provision of technical assistance and other supports over the course of its first 12 months of operation, before being permanently relocated to the providers' homes.

The state of Kansas, meanwhile, recently dedicated $94 million in COVID relief funding to the creation of more than 6,400 new child care slots via a pair of innovative accelerator projects: a Capital Projects Fund Accelerator, designed to help build or renovate facilities creating new licensed care, and a Child Care Capacity Accelerator, designed to support operational logistics and business sustainability solutions (Jirgens, 2024).

Solving the Workforce Crisis

Perhaps most promising of all is a recent initiative, Power to the Profession, designed to define, transform, and unify the early childhood profession—which, as you've learned, currently encompasses a wide array of professionals employed by an equally diverse collection of programs and service provision types. Created through an extensive consensus-building process among 15 national early childhood organizations, the Power to the Profession Task Force's (2020) final report, the *Unifying Framework for the Early Childhood Profession*, offers a road map to a future in which early childhood educators are respected and professionally compensated in conjunction with a first-of-its-kind, three-tiered licensure structure designed for interstate operability.

Released just weeks before the onset of the COVID-19 pandemic, the Unifying Framework is now gaining momentum, with the recent Connecticut Blue Ribbon Panel on Child Care (2023) recommending its first-ever statewide implementation in a move that could transform the profession for the better across decades to come.

The Path Forward: Knowing Better and Doing Better

As we wrap up our conversation, I want to take just a moment to reiterate why I wrote this book and what I hope it might help to accomplish. If you take nothing else away from our time together, let it be this: *The early years are uniquely consequential—and infinitely more important than our nation's public policy might lead you to believe.*

My hope in writing this book has been to help right that wrong, to arm you with the information that you might need as a policymaker, parent, or early childhood professional to take action within your own sphere of influence. So, in place of this chapter's Bipartisan Blueprint for Change section, I'd like to close out with a word of advice common to all three groups best captured in a quote commonly attributed to poet Maya Angelou, though existing in multiple variations since at least 1910 (Quote Investigator, 2022).

The Angelou version (supposedly conveyed as personal advice to television host Oprah Winfrey, who had been lamenting poor decisions she made early in life) goes like this:

> You did what you knew how to do, and when you knew better, you did better.

This idea of tying action to knowledge has always had special appeal to me. In much of life, we act on the basis of cultural norms and popular wisdom. The associated peer pressure can be powerful—not leading us actively astray as much as creating conditions in which we never even pause to question widely held assumptions. Until we know better, that is . . . at which point we are all called to act.

It is my sincere hope that having engaged with this book, you now *know better* when it comes to the value of the early years and the brokenness of our associated systems and policies.

What happens next is up to you.

Interpreting Claims About Early Childhood Research

Chapter 2's discussion of some of the early childhood field's landmark studies struck me as a perfect opportunity to pause and address a topic you're almost certain to run into the deeper you dive into the world of early childhood policy. That is the selective interpretation of early childhood's published research base, which has become all too pervasive in ideological circles.

Especially if you're a policymaker, it's likely you've been exposed to hyperbolic—and demonstrably false—claims suggesting that "Head Start doesn't work," that "a study from Tennessee proves that prekindergarten is a waste," or that "the benefits of early childhood interventions fade out by the third grade."

This quick aside is hardly the place to begin debunking these claims systematically, but I did want to say a few words about critical literacy when it comes to such assertions, many of which pluck individual data points from far more complex analyses and then assert them as the final word on a topic—even when contradicted by similar, more recent, and/or better constructed studies.

Across decades of published research, it is absolutely true that individual studies have produced unexpected and even negative program outcomes when assessed against specific measures. But an overemphasis on individual data points captured in these studies often conveniently (and sometimes deliberately) overlooks more positive findings—often located in the very same publications.

Children who do not have preschool experiences may in fact catch up on certain discrete academic skills by the 3rd grade, for example, but it's important to remember both that life doesn't end at age 8 and that the value of these investments isn't limited to a specific measure of literacy, or even test scores at a single grade level. To suggest that the benefits of early investment fade out in the 3rd grade is to willfully ignore an ever-growing body of evidence to the contrary, as well as the significant longitudinal (and even multigenerational) findings described in Chapter 2. Likewise, a single state's poorly implemented prekindergarten program does not negate dozens of positive counterexamples from states across the nation.

Is early investment a silver bullet, capable of decisively counteracting all of the world's ills? No. But when it comes to research claims, do your own homework, and consider findings consistent across multiple studies.

Reaching Out to Your Elected Leaders

A How-To for Parents and Professionals

As someone who has spent more than 2 decades working closely with state-level policymakers, I recognize that some of this book's advice around policymaker outreach may still seem a little vague and intimidating to readers who do not regularly interact with elected leaders and their staff. But it's not as difficult or daunting as it may seem. If you'd like a little more detailed guidance here—some real brass tacks on how to find and contact policymakers—read on.

IDENTIFYING YOUR STATE'S ELECTED LEADERS

As a general rule of thumb, there are three state-level elected leaders—who must rely on your vote personally—to whom *your voice* holds a particular place of importance in the world of policy. The first is *your state's governor*. The remaining two are the *state legislators* elected to represent your specific place of residence/business. (State lawmakers represent finite geographic districts within each state, whereas statewide officials such as governors represent all of a state's citizens independent of geography.)

With the exception of Nebraska, which is home to the country's only unicameral (or single-chambered) legislature, each state legislature is home to two separate chambers: a comparatively larger *House of Representatives* (known alternately in some states as a State Assembly or House of Delegates) and a comparatively smaller *State Senate*. (Nebraska has only a Senate.)

How do you identify your personal House and Senate members? The Internet is your friend here. Visit your preferred search engine, enter the name of your state and "state legislature," and connect to your state's legislative website, almost all of which allow you to search for your personal elected leaders by entering your address or zip code.

If your state doesn't offer such search functionality, search for a map of your state's House and Senate legislative districts to determine which you reside in (these are usually numbered) and then go back and cross-reference elected leaders by district. Don't forget that you want to identify *both* your representative (assembly member or delegate) and your senator. Because these districts are not always the same (Senate districts are typically larger), you may have to conduct this mapping exercise twice.

Identifying your state's governor is just as easy. Enter your state name and "governor" into your search engine, and their office's contact information should pull right up.

CALLING YOUR STATE LAWMAKERS

Unlike calling your governor's office (in which a direct connection to the governor is highly unlikely), outreach to your state lawmakers may or may not result in an immediate personal conversation. During off-hours and depending on available staffing, it's not unheard of for lawmakers to field office calls personally (so be prepared, should opportunity knock)—though chances are good that you will initially reach a staff member or voicemail. Should you reach a voicemail or someone other than your lawmaker, I'd strongly encourage you *not to share the full content of your message via voicemail* and call it a day. Instead, try to arrange for an actual conversation. Should you reach a particularly helpful staff member, feel free to share your story with them, but as a preface to (and not in place of) a direct connection with your elected official.

Here are a few tips for this initial conversation:

- Always refer to your lawmaker by their official title (e.g., "Senator Brown" or "Representative Smith").
- Be sure to clearly identify yourself, not only by name but by address as well. State lawmakers may receive outreach from dozens (or more) callers daily, often from individuals living outside of their districts who are calling *all lawmakers*. But *you* are special in this case. When calling your own personal lawmakers, you are a voter in their district, a constituent for

whom responsive service is paramount. So make sure they know you're in this category when it applies.

- Ask for a call back or, better yet, ask to schedule an appointment to speak with your lawmaker.
- Note, too, that some legislative websites will list both a lawmaker's legislative office contacts and their home/business contacts. Don't be shy about using these secondary resources. In most cases, elected service is a part-time role, separate from a lawmaker's full-time occupation, which means that for many there are entire months of the year during which they may not be a daily presence at your state capitol. (Remember: If they weren't comfortable being contacted at home or their primary place of business, they wouldn't have posted this information.) Just use it respectfully (between 9 a.m. and 5 p.m.) and recognize that you're much more likely to reach your lawmaker directly using these contacts, which are frequently cell phone numbers, so be prepared. (Recognizing that you may be reaching them during work or time with family, it's always respectful to introduce yourself briefly and inquire whether this is a good time for them to speak, or if they'd prefer you set a time for a follow-up conversation.)

Here's an example of what an initial call could sound like:

Good morning, my name is (NAME), and I was hoping to speak with Senator Brown.
    Might they be available?

If asked to leave a message or if you reach their voicemail directly, try something like this (adapting, of course, to your own personal details and message):

My name is Dan Wuori, and I am a constituent of Senator Brown's. I am the owner of the Spring Valley Learning Academy at 1234 Sparkleberry Lane. We are a preschool program serving 68 children ages 6 weeks to 4 years. I was hoping to schedule an appointment with the Senator to discuss some concerns I have about the state's subsidy reimbursement rates, which are having a very negative impact on my ability to hire and compensate qualified teachers. I know this is an issue important to the Senator. I can be reached at . . .

CALLING YOUR STATE GOVERNOR

When calling your governor's office, you'll need to take a little different approach. Here it's highly unlikely that you'll connect initially (or possibly ever) with the governor, who—unlike your House and Senate members—represents your entire state. This means that you'll almost certainly begin by speaking to a staff member . . . but it needn't be the general receptionist. Here, ask to be connected to the *policy advisor responsible for overseeing the administration's early childhood/child care programming*. This call, with the general switchboard, may go something like this:

> My name is Dan Wuori, and I am a child care business owner in (YOUR CITY). I was hoping, first, that you might be able to tell me who on the governor's staff is responsible for overseeing child care issues . . . and then connect me with (or allow me to leave a message for) that person . . .

KNOW WHO HAS "THE JUICE"

While it is always wise and beneficial to contact your personal elected leaders, know that not all power and influence is distributed equally within legislative settings. Because the legislative process generally runs through committees in each chamber (House and Senate), the members of these committees often have an outsized role in shaping topical policy that may exceed that of your individual House member or Senator.

If you are monitoring specific legislation, it is helpful to know which committees will have the greatest say in issues related (in this case) to children and families and who the members of these committees are. Here again, your state's legislative website is a great tool, but don't overlook the value of your personal elected officials and their staff in helping to guide you here. This is as simple as a call and can often be resolved by the staff member answering the phone. Simply ask which committee would generally oversee issues related to child care, for example.

Know in advance that the Daycare Myth is alive and well in most state legislatures, with responsibility for issues related to young children routinely split between education committees (which generally oversee issues related to the state's public school systems) and health/human services committees (which, in many states, continue to govern child care as a service separate and distinct from education . . . *sigh*). Given child care's status as a business and its relationship to workforce participation, it is also not uncommon for related legislation to be taken up by committees handling commerce and business interests. These committees vary in name and structure by state, but with a little digging you should be able to identify them readily. If you know a specific bill number, you can also search it on most legislative websites and identify the committee(s) to which it has been assigned.

Note that while new legislation generally passes through this topical committee structure, many early childhood policies are enacted via state budgets. Here you'll want to explore membership on House and Senate finance committees (sometimes called appropriations or ways and means).

In the event that you're making outreach to lawmakers for whom you are not a direct constituent, you'll still want to identify your city of residence, but explain that you are contacting them in their capacity as a committee member.

WHEN YOU CONNECT

Finally, as you prepare for these conversations themselves, here are a few guiding questions to ask yourself that will assist in relaying your concerns. Only you will know the answers to these questions (as related to your family or business), but hopefully they'll provide some food for thought as you consider what you want to share. Above all else, know that your story matters.

Parents

- What has been your experience in trying to identify affordable, high-quality early care and education in your community? How has this experience varied, according to the age of your child? (Did you have particular difficulty finding an infant placement, for example?)
- How is the price of child care impacting your family? What, if any, sacrifices are you making? How does this monthly cost compare to other significant expenses like your rent/mortgage?

- How do you feel about the quality of the programs you've been able to find? Likewise, how did you feel about the array of choices available to you in making your selection? Did you have multiple, public, and private options from which to choose—or did income, geography, or other factors limit your available choices? If you receive a child care subsidy, has the state's reimbursement rate limited your choices and/or added burden to your family budget in the form of high co-payments?
- How many times have teaching staff members in your child's classroom departed from their roles to take other jobs? If you know the answer, where did they go and why? (Did they leave child care altogether?) How is the compensation for these teachers (or, more often, a lack thereof) impacting your child's experience?
- How do you feel about the number of children in your child's classroom? Are adult:child ratios sufficient to provide your child with the type of individualized attention and care needed to optimize their development, or do teachers seem overwhelmed?
- Are you happy about your current caregiving arrangement? Given different resources, might you have preferred to either (a) participate in the workforce rather than staying at home with your child, or (b) stay at home with your child as opposed to relying on external supports?
- If you qualify for a child care subsidy, prekindergarten, or other publicly funded programs, have you actually been able to access them? If not, why? If so, what was the application process like, how long did you have to wait, and how are these services making a difference for your family?

Professionals

- How are things going for your business at this moment? Are you thriving? Struggling to keep the doors open? Take a moment to reflect on your current situation and tell your story. If actions taken or policies enacted on behalf of your state are influencing your business (for better or worse), be prepared to share this part of your story. What could the state do to better ensure your success?

- If applicable, how has the entry of school districts into your local early childhood marketplace (for the provision of prekindergarten, for example) impacted the stability of your business, your enrollment, the rates you charge, your ability to hire and retain staff, and/or your ability to provide care to infants and toddlers? Is your business able to participate in the state's mixed-delivery system as a prekindergarten provider? If not, what barriers to entry are you experiencing?
- Does your business enroll children receiving child care subsidies? If so, how does the rate currently offered by the state compare to that paid by unsubsidized parents? What are the implications of this diminished rate on your program's quality and ability to compensate and retain teachers? If your program does not accept state subsidies, why? What could the state do differently to encourage your participation?
- What is your current experience with hiring and retention? What hourly rates are you able to offer staff, and how do these rates compare to other employment options in your community? Do you offer health and retirement benefits? If not, why is this a challenge, and how does it impact staffing? Do you have current staffing vacancies? If so, how long is it taking to fill them and how do you feel about the applicant pools?
- Are you currently operating at full capacity? If not, to what do you attribute this situation? Do you have vacancies caused by staffing shortages?
- How does your state's regulatory environment impact your operations and profitability? Are there administrative barriers that could be removed without impacting the safety and quality of your program? If so, what are they?

References

Ackerman, S. (1992). *Discovering the brain.* National Academies Press.

American Academy of Pediatrics. (2022). *Breastfeeding: AAP policy explained.* https://www.healthychildren.org/English/ages-stages/baby/breastfeed ing/Pages/Where-We-Stand-Breastfeeding.aspx

Anbar-Shaheen, R. (2022). *DC announces free health insurance for child care workers and their families.* Under 3 DC. https://under3dc.org/healthcareforchild careworkers/

Annie E. Casey Foundation. (2023). *Child well-being in single-parent families.* https://www.aecf.org/blog/child-well-being-in-single-parent-families

Bipartisan Policy Center. (2019). *History of federal funding for child care and early learning.* https://bipartisanpolicy.org/download/?file=/wp-content/uploads /2019/10/WEB_BPC_ECH-History-Brief_R01.pdf

Bipartisan Policy Center. (2020a). *Paid family leave in the United States: A primer on working family trends and paid family leave.* https://bipartisanpolicy.org /download/?file=/wp-content/uploads/2020/02/Paid-Family-Leave-in -the-United-States.pdf

Bipartisan Policy Center. (2020b). *The limitations of using market rates for setting child care subsidy rates.* https://bipartisanpolicy.org/download/?file=/wp -content/uploads/2020/06/Limitations_of_Market_Rate_Surveys_for _Child_Care_Brief_FINAL1.pdf

Bishop, S. (2023). *$122 billion: The growing, annual cost of the infant-toddler child care crisis.* Ready Nation/Council for a Strong America. https://strongnation .s3.amazonaws.com/documents/1598/05d917e2-9618-4648-a0ee -1b35d17e2a4d.pdf?1674854626&inline;%20filename=%22$122%20 Billion:%20The%20Growing,%20Annual%20Cost%20of%20the%20 Infant-Toddler%20Child%20Care%20Crisis.pdf%22

Boushey, H., Barrow, L., Goda, G. S., Lee, V., Pasnau, A., & Wheaton, S. (2022). *Care businesses: A model that doesn't work for providers, workers, or families.* The White House. https://www.whitehouse.gov/cea/written-materials /2022/04/08/care-businesses-a-model-that-doesnt-work-for-providers -workers-or-families/

Brain Architecture. (n.d.). Harvard Center on the Developing Child. https:// developingchild.harvard.edu/science/key-concepts/brain-architecture/

Brito, N. H., Werchan, D., Brandes-Aitken, A., Yoshikawa, H., Greaves, A., & Zhang, M. (2022). Paid maternal leave is associated with infant brain function at 3 months of age. *Child Development, 93*(4),1030–1043.

Budig, M. (2014). *The fatherhood bonus and the motherhood penalty: Parenthood and the gender gap in pay.* Third Way. https://www.thirdway.org/report/the-fatherhood-bonus-and-the-motherhood-penalty-parenthood-and-the-gender-gap-in-pay

Campbell, F., Conti, G., Heckman, J. J., Moon, S. H., Pinto, R., Pungello, E., & Pan, Y. (2014). Early childhood investments substantially boost adult health. *Science, 343*(6178), 1478–1485.

Center for American Progress. (2018). *Child care access in the United States.* https://childcaredeserts.org/2018/

Center for the Study of Child Care Employment. (2021). *Early Childhood Workforce Index 2020.* University of California, Berkeley. https://cscce.berkeley.edu/workforce-index-2020/wp-content/uploads/sites/3/2021/02/Early-Childhood-Workforce-Index-2020.pdf

Centers for Disease Control and Prevention. (2023). *Breastfeeding: Why it matters.* United States Centers for Disease Control and Prevention. https://www.cdc.gov/breastfeeding/about-breastfeeding/why-it-matters.html

Chai, Y., Nandi, A., & Heymann, J. (2018). Does extending the duration of legislated paid maternity leave improve breastfeeding practices? Evidence from 38 low-income and middle-income countries. *BMJ Global Health, 3*(5), e001032.

Child Care and Development Block Grant Act of 2014 (CCDBG), Pub. L. No. 113–186, November 19, 2014. https://www.congress.gov/113/plaws/publ186/PLAW-113publ186.pdf

Child Care Aware of America. (2022). *Demanding change: Repairing our child care system.* https://www.childcareaware.org/demanding-change-repairing-our-child-care-system/

Clear, J. (2018). *Atomic habits: An easy & proven way to build good habits & break bad ones.* Avery Publishing.

Connecticut Blue Ribbon Panel on Child Care. (2023). *Blue Ribbon Panel on Child Care report.* Connecticut Office of Early Childhood. https://www.ctoec.org/blue-ribbon-panel/

Covert, B. (2022). *New Mexico just became the first state to make child care free for nearly all families.* Early Learning Nation. https://earlylearningnation.com/2022/05/new-mexico-just-became-the-first-state-to-make-child-care-free-for-nearly-all-families/

Daugherty, L., Nguyen, P., Kushner, J., & Riley Bahr, P. (2023). *How to build stackable credentials.* Rand Corporation. https://www.rand.org/pubs/commentary/2023/10/how-to-build-stackable-credentials.html

de Bellefonds, C. (2021). *When your baby can hear in the womb.* What to Expect. https://www.whattoexpect.com/pregnancy/fetal-development/fetal-hearing/

DiPalma, B. (2023). *As Walmart, Home Depot raise wages, analyst calls it 'no brainer' for long-term value.* Yahoo Finance. https://finance.yahoo.com/news/as-walmart-home-depot-raise-wages-analyst-calls-it-no-brainer-for-long-term-value-204123193.html

Duffort, L. (2023). *Lawmakers pass bill to make 'quantum leap' in child care investments.* The VT Digger. https://vtdigger.org/2023/05/12/lawmakers-pass-bill-to-make-quantum-leap-in-child-care-investments/

Early Learning PA Coalition. (2023). *It's unanimous! 98% of PA voters believe early childhood education is important.* https://www.prekforpa.org/its-unanimous-98-of-pa-voters-believe-early-childhood-education-is-important/

Eckenrode, J., Campa, M., Luckey, D. W., Henderson, C. R. Jr., Cole, R., Kitzman, H., Anson, E., Sidora-Arcoleo, K., Powers, J., & Olds, D. (2010). Long-term effects of prenatal and infancy nurse home visitation on the life course of youths: 19-year follow-up of a randomized trial. *Archives of Pediatric and Adolescent Medicine, 164*(1), 9–15.

Edwards, C. (2023). *Cutting federal farm subsidies.* The Cato Institute. https://www.cato.org/briefing-paper/cutting-federal-farm-subsidies

ElHage, A. (2022). *5 questions with family studies: Katharine Stevens on family-focused child care policy.* Institute for Family Studies. https://ifstudies.org/blog/5-questions-with-family-studies-katharine-stevens-on-family-focused-child-care-policy

First Five Years Fund. (2022). *President leads with child care & pre-K in meeting with major CEOs.* https://www.ffyf.org/2022/01/24/1-in-3-child-care-workers-is-experiencing-food-insecurity/

First Five Years Fund. (2023). *The first five things to know about: A new poll showing voter support for child care funding.* https://www.ffyf.org/july23poll

Funke, D. (2021). *Fact check: Build Back Better Act includes more than $2 trillion in spending, tax cuts.* USA Today. https://www.usatoday.com/story/news/factcheck/2021/12/07/fact-check-missing-context-claim-cost-build-back-better/8843153002/

Garcia, J., Bennhoff, F., Leaf, D., & Heckman, J. (2021). *The dynastic benefits of early childhood education.* University of Chicago. https://bfi.uchicago.edu/wp-content/uploads/2021/06/BFI_WP_2021-77.pdf

Garcia, J., Heckman, J., Leaf, D., & Prados, M. (2017). *Quantifying the life-cycle benefits of a prototypical early childhood program.* Heckman Equation. https://heckmanequation.org/wp-content/uploads/2017/12/abc_comprehensivecba_JPE-SUBMISSION_2017-05-26a_sjs_sjs.pdf

Gascon, C. (2023). *Are parents' labor participation rates returning to pre-pandemic levels?* Federal Reserve Bank of St. Louis. https://www.stlouisfed.org/on-the-economy/2023/apr/parents-labor-participation-rates-returning-pre-pandemic-levels

Goldstein, D. (2022). *Can child care be a big business? Private equity thinks so.* The New York Times. https://www.nytimes.com/2022/12/16/us/child-care-centers-private-equity.html

Goss-Graves, F. (2021). *The roots of our child care crisis are in the legacy of slavery.* The Hill. https://thehill.com/changing-america/opinion/559457-the-roots -of-our-child-care-crisis-are-in-the-legacy-of-slavery/

Grunewald, R., & Davies, P. (2011). *Hardly child's play: Times have been even rougher than usual for district child care providers.* Minneapolis Federal Reserve Bank. https://www.minneapolisfed.org/article/2011/hardly-childs -play

Hayes, T., & Kerska, K. (2021). *Primer: Agriculture subsidies and their influence on the composition of U.S. food supply and consumption.* American Action Forum. https://www.americanactionforum.org/research/primer-agriculture-sub sidies-and-their-influence-on-the-composition-of-u-s-food-supply-and -consumption/

Heckman, J. J. (2006). Skill formation and the economics of investing in disadvantaged children. *Science, 312*(5782), 1900–1902.

Heckman, J. J. (2019). *Early childhood education strengthens families and can break the cycle of poverty.* Perry Preschool: Intergenerational Effects. https:// heckmanequation.org/wp-content/uploads/2019/05/F_Heckman _PerryMidlife_OnePager_050819.pdf

Heckman, J. J., Moon, S. E., Pinto, R., Savelyev, P. A., & Yavitz, A. (2010). The rate of return to the HighScope Perry Preschool Program. *Journal of Public Economics, 94*(1–2), 114–128.

Hepper, P. G. (1988). Fetal "soap" addiction. *Lancet, 1*(8598), 1347–1348. http:// doi.org/10.1016/s0140-6736(88)92170-8

The Hunt Institute. (2021a). *Child care and prekindergarten in the Build Back Better Act: A guide for policymakers.* https://hunt-institute.org/resources/2021/11 /build-back-better-guide-for-policymakers-early-childhood-education/

The Hunt Institute. (2021b). *COVID-19: State child care actions.* https://hunt -institute.org/covid-19-resources/state-child-care-actions-covid-19/

The Hunt Institute. (2022). *The Child Care and Development Grant Block Grant Reauthorization Act of 2022: A guide for policymakers.* https://hunt-institute .org/resources/2022/03/the-child-care-and-development-block-grant -reauthorization-act-of-2022-a-guide-for-policymakers-early-childhood -education/

Jirgens, A. (2024). *Kansas governor announces nearly $28 million to create 458 child care slots, new community facilities.* KAKE TV. https://www.kake.com/story /50426710/kansas-governor-announces-nearly-dollar28-million-to -create-458-child-care-slots-new-community-facilities

KAKE (ABC Television). (2022). *'It's the hardest decision': El Dorado daycare closes as child care staff shortages reach crisis levels.* KAKE TV. https://www.kake .com/story/47138097/its-the-hardest-decision-el-dorado-daycare-closes -as-child-care-staff-shortages-reach-crisis-levels

Khater, S., McManus, D., & Karamon, K. (2020). *Family budget burdens squeezing housing: Child care costs.* Freddie Mac. https://www.freddiemac.com /research/insight/20200107-family-budget-burdens

Kids Count Data Center. (2021a). *Births to women receiving late or no prenatal care in United States.* Annie E. Casey Foundation. https://datacenter.aecf.org/data /tables/11-births-to-women-receiving-late-or-no-prenatal-care#detailed/1 /any/false/2048,574,1729,37,871,870,573,869,36,868/any/265,266

Kids Count Data Center. (2021b). *Children under age 6 with all available parents in the labor force in United States.* Annie E. Casey Foundation. https:// datacenter.aecf.org/data/tables/5057-children-under-age-6-with-all -available-parents-in-the-labor-force

LeBerte, J. (2023). *Alabama Department of Human Resources offers additional funding to child care providers.* Alabama Public Radio. https://www.apr.org /news/2023-07-11/alabama-department-of-human-resources-offers -additional-funding-to-child-care-providers

Mariani, B., Nicoletti, G., Barzon, G., Clemencia Ortiz Barajas, M., Shukla, M., Guevara, R., Simon Suweis, S., and Gervain, J. (2023). *Prenatal experience with language shapes the brain.* Science Advances. https://www.science.org /doi/10.1126/sciadv.adj3524

McCarthy, K. (2023). *Fast-food workers in California to earn $20 an hour in 2024.* ABC News. https://abcnews.go.com/GMA/Food/fast-food-workers -california-earn-20-hour-highest/story?id=103593696

McElroy, M. (2013). *While in womb, babies begin learning language from their mothers.* University of Washington. https://www.washington.edu/news /2013/01/02/while-in-womb-babies-begin-learning-language-from -their-mothers/

McGinn, D., & Posnanski, J. (2019). *Mike Petters leads the largest military ship-builder in the United States. His top national security issue? It's not what you might think.* The Business Journals. https://www.bizjournals.com/bizjournals/ne ws/2019/01/31/mike-petters-leads-the-largest-military.html

Mencken, H. L. (1920). *Prejudices: Second series.* Alfred A. Knopf.

Miller, T. R. (2015). Projected outcomes of Nurse-Family Partnership home visitation during 1996–2013, USA. *Prevention Science, 16*(6), 765–777.

Minnesota Statutes. (2023). At home infant child care program, Section 199B.035. https://www.revisor.mn.gov/statutes/cite/119B.035

National Public Radio. (2001). *Conservative advocate.* Morning Edition. https:// www.npr.org/templates/story/story.php?storyId=1123439

National Women's Business Council. (2020). *National Women's Business Council annual report, 2020.* https://www.nwbc.gov/report/2020-annual-report/

National Women's Law Center. (2023). *States can make care less taxing.* https:// nwlc.org/wp-content/uploads/2023/03/MakingCareLessTaxingFS.pdf

Nestle, M. (1993). Food lobbies, the food pyramid, and U.S. nutrition policy. *International Journal of Health Services, 23*(3), 483–496. http://doi.org/10 .2190/32F2-2PFB-MEG7-8HPU

New Mexico Early Childhood Education and Care Department. (2023). *Pre-K pay parity for early childhood educators.* https://ececdscholarship.org/wage -parity-information/

Norton, R. (n.d.). *Unintended consequences.* Econlib. https://www.econlib.org
/library/Enc/UnintendedConsequences.html

Nurse-Family Partnership. (2017). *Nurse-family partnership: Outcomes, costs and
return on investment in the U.S.* https://www.nursefamilypartnership.org/wp
-content/uploads/2017/02/Miller-State-Specific-Fact-Sheet_US
_20170405-1.pdf

Nurse-Family Partnership. (2022). *Nurse-family partnership: Research trials and
outcomes.* https://www.nursefamilypartnership.org/wp-content/uploads
/2022/03/NFP-Research-Trials-and-Outcomes.pdf

Office of New Mexico Governor Michelle Lujan Grisham. (2022). *Gov. Lujan
Grisham announces historic pay increase for early childhood workforce.* https://
www.governor.state.nm.us/2022/10/06/gov-lujan-grisham-announces
-historic-pay-increase-for-early-childhood-workforce/

O'Hara, M. (2023). *State finalizes new child care assistance rules.* Santa Fe New
Mexican. https://www.santafenewmexican.com/news/education/state
-finalizes-new-child-care-assistance-rules/article_39a2ec5e-2717-11ee
-9f21-9b3b8fd48fdc.html

Partanen, E., Kujala, T., Tervaniemi, M., & Huotilainen, M. (2013). Prenatal
music exposure induces long-term neural effects. *PloS One, 8*(10), e78946.

Patel, B. (2023). *The U.S. states where childcare costs more than college tuition.* Net-
Credit. https://www.netcredit.com/blog/cost-of-child-care-by-state/

Petters, M. (2019). *Mike Petters, remarks as prepared, for the early childhood leadership summit.* https://hunt-institute.org/resources/2019/06/mike-petters
-remarks-as-prepared-for-the-early-childhood-leadership-summit/

Powell, L. (2022). *What we learned about Michigan's child care crisis from parents
and providers.* Muckrock. https://www.muckrock.com/news/archives/2022
/aug/29/what-we-learned-michigan-childcare-providers/

Power to the Profession Task Force. (2020). *Unifying framework for the early childhood education profession.* https://powertotheprofession.org/wp-content
/uploads/2020/03/Power-to-Profession-Framework-exec-summary
-03082020.pdf

Putterman, A. (2024). *Amid child care crisis, advocates hope to expand CT pilot program that helps parents run day cares.* CT Insider. https://www.ctinsider.com
/news/article/ct-child-care-incubator-pilot-expansion-18585071.php

Pyanov, M. (2023). *The Food Pyramid and obesity | 3 major mistakes made.* Belly-
Belly. https://www.bellybelly.com.au/general-health/food-pyramid/

Quote Investigator. (2022). *You did what you knew how to do, and when you knew
better, you did better.* Quote Investigator. https://quoteinvestigator.com/2022
/11/30/did-better/

Reynolds, A. J., Temple, J. A., Ou, S. R., Robertson, D. L., Mersky, J. P., Topitzes,
J. W., & Niles, M. D. (2007). Effects of a school-based, early childhood intervention on adult health and well-being: A 19-year follow-up of low-income
families. *Archives of Pediatric and Adolescent Medicine, 161*(8), 730–739.

Royal, J., & O'Shea, A. (2023). *What is the average stock market return?* Nerd-Wallet. https://www.nerdwallet.com/article/investing/average-stock-mar ket-return

Rush, C. (2022). *'Desperation': Child care struggle worsens in rural U.S.* Associated Press. https://apnews.com/article/inflation-health-education-covid-child -care-837040ecd097d67aa00c2d178ea0e659

Schweinhart, L. J. (2005). *The HighScope Perry Preschool study through age 40.* High Scope Educational Research Foundation. https://highscope.org/wp-con tent/uploads/2018/11/perry-preschool-summary-40.pdf

Smith, A. (2015). *The long-run effects of universal pre-K on criminal activity.* Society of Labor Economists. https://papers.ssrn.com/sol3/papers.cfm?abstract _id=2685507

Smith, L., Suenaga, M., & Campbell, M. (2020). *Demystifying child care affordability.* Bipartisan Policy Center. https://bipartisanpolicy.org/blog/demys tifying-child-care-affordability/

Stampfer, M. J., & Willett, W. C. (2006). *Rebuilding the Food Pyramid.* Scientific American. https://www.scientificamerican.com/article/rebuilding-the-food -pyramid/

Stevens, K., & Weidinger, M. (2021). *Improving early childhood development by allowing advanced child tax credits.* American Enterprise Institute. https:// www.aei.org/research-products/report/improving-early-childhood -development-by-allowing-advanced-child-tax-credits/

Sutherland, P., & Chakrabarti, M. (2023). *How to save child care in the face of a massive funding loss.* WBUR. https://www.wbur.org/onpoint/2023/09/13 /how-to-save-childcare-in-the-face-of-a-massive-funding-loss

Tate Sullivan, E. (2021). *The pandemic has compounded the turnover problem in early childhood education.* EdSurge. https://www.edsurge.com/news/2021 -02-09-the-pandemic-has-compounded-the-turnover-problem-in-early -childhood-education

Thier, J. (2022). *The cost of child care has risen by 41% during the pandemic with families spending up to 20% of their salaries.* Fortune Magazine. https://fortune .com/2022/01/28/the-cost-of-child-care-in-the-us-is-rising/

Troller-Renfree, S. V., Costanzo, M. A., Duncan, G. J., Magnuson, K., Gennetian, L. A., Yoshikawa, H., Halpern-Meekin, S., Fox, N. A., & Noble, K. G. (2022). The impact of poverty reduction intervention on infant brain activity. *Proceedings of the National Academy of Sciences, 119*(5), e2115649119.

U.S. Bureau of Labor Statistics. (2022). *2022 Occupational outlook handbook.* U.S. Bureau of Labor Statistics. https://www.bls.gov/ooh/

U.S. Census Bureau. (2020). *2018 CBP and NES Combined Report.* https://www .census.gov/data/tables/2018/econ/cbp/2018-combined-report.html

U.S. Department of Health and Human Services, Office of Child Care. (2023). *Child care and development fund payment rates.* https://www.acf.hhs.gov/occ /news/child-care-and-development-fund-payment-rates

U.S. Department of Justice. (2023). *Census Bureau median family income by family size.* https://www.justice.gov/ust/eo/bapcpa/20230401/bci_data/median _income_table.htm

U.S. Government Accountability Office. (2021). *Child care: Subsidy eligibility and receipt, and wait lists (GAO-21-245R).* https://www.gao.gov/products/gao-21 -245r

Weil, J. Z., & Brice-Saddler, M. (2021). *D.C. votes to raise taxes on the rich.* The Washington Post. https://www.washingtonpost.com/local/dc-politics/dc -council-tax-increase-budget/2021/07/20/36f483d4-e8e7-11eb-97a0 -a09d10181e36_story.html

Weisshaar, K. (2018). From opt out to blocked out: The challenges for labor market re-entry after family-related employment lapses. *American Sociological Review, 83*(1), 34–60.

Wong, R. (2022). *Free preschool delayed for thousands of Oregon children due in part to staffing shortages.* The Oregonian. https://www.oregonlive.com/education /2022/12/free-preschool-delayed-for-thousands-of-oregon-children-due -in-part-to-staffing-shortages.html

Index

About the Author

Dan Wuori is the founder and president of Early Childhood Policy Solutions LLC (a public policy consultancy focused on the needs of young children and families) and strategic advisor on Early Childhood at the Saul Zaentz Charitable Foundation. Recognized internationally as an expert in early childhood development and policy, he is an accomplished author, public speaker, and trusted policy advisor to America's governors, state lawmakers, and other senior officials.

Dr. Wuori joined The Hunt Institute as its founding director of early learning in January 2019, and he served as senior director from February 2021 to November 2023, helping to attract more than $10 million in philanthropic and fee-for-service work to the institute.

A former kindergarten teacher and school district administrator, Dr. Wuori served as deputy director of South Carolina First Steps to School Readiness—the state's comprehensive, public-private early learning initiative—from 2005 to 2018. In this role, he worked alongside elected leaders to develop significant bipartisan support for early childhood education and oversaw system innovations, including the delivery of public prekindergarten in private, community- and faith-based preschools, improvements to the state's IDEA Part C early intervention system, the creation of statewide program accountability standards, and the expansion of evidence-based home visiting programs.

Dr. Wuori lives in Columbia, South Carolina, with his wife and two children.